HORIZON

AUTUMN, 1975 • VOLUME XVII, NUMBER 4

HORIZON

AUTUMN, 1975 • VOLUME XVII, NUMBER 4

HORIZON is published every three months by American Heritage Publishing Co., Inc. Editorial and executive offices: 1221 Avenue of the Americas, New York, N.Y. 10020. Treasurer: Marjorie C. Dyer. Secretary: William Cusick. All correspondence about subscriptions should be addressed to: HORIZON Subscription Office, 379 West Center St., Marion, Ohio 43302.

Single copies: $7.50. Subscriptions: $26.00 per year in the U.S.; Canada and elsewhere $28.00.

Cumulative indexes for Volumes I–V, VI–X, and XI–XV are available at $5. HORIZON is also indexed in the *Readers' Guide to Periodical Literature.* The editors welcome contributions but can assume no responsibility for unsolicited material. Title registered U.S. Patent Office. Second-class postage paid at New York, N.Y., and at additional mailing offices.

End of the Innocent Bystander

The cluster of articles on the history of famine (beginning on page 32) is not likely to inspire much optimism. The experts are apparently agreed that there is enough food in the world to go around, yet the obstacles, chiefly political, to redistributing even a minor fraction of it seem all but insurmountable. And though much has been heard about the Green Revolution, it has problems aplenty, too. The new high-yield grains, despite their impressive success in Mexico and elsewhere, require so much water, fertilizer, and cultivation that many of the people who need them most simply can't afford to grow them.

These are among the reasons that, of the earth's 3.6 billion inhabitants, half a billion still haven't enough to eat. This is also why an increasing number of people believe that any solution to the problem has to be more radical than has been envisioned so far, and that it is going to have to come not from government but from ourselves. As the theologian Halford Luccock has observed, "One of the prominent figures of history has died, the 'innocent bystander.' "

One group that clearly agrees is the New Alchemy Institute on Cape Cod. Begun five years ago on a small farm near Falmouth, this ecological experiment consists of some eighteen researchers who think our agricultural technology is headed for disaster, perhaps within ten or twenty years. As evidence, they point to the steadily rising prices of fertilizer and fuel and to the cumulative biological damage caused by the fertilizers, pesticides, fungicides, and herbicides upon which modern agriculture depends. John Todd, a marine biologist now at the Institute, calls the Green Revolution "the agricultural equivalent of the launching of the *Titanic*." According to Todd, for all its newness, the Green Revolution (whose keenest enthusiasts are usually manufacturers of chemicals and tractors) merely exports an agricultural technology that relies heavily on natural gas and

petroleum, two perilously finite resources. The only solution, he and his colleagues are persuaded, is through some quite different way of producing food.

This is where the New Alchemy Institute's arks, as they call them, come in. An ark consists of three ponds at different levels. In the topmost pond, bacteria convert ammonia from fish wastes into nitrates and nitrites that serve as food for algae in the pond. Water containing these algae flows into the middle pond, where water fleas eat some of the algae. Then the water, full of fleas and the remaining algae, flows into the bottom pond, carrying with it a complete diet for three kinds of fish—tilapia, white amur, and mirror carp. Last year one of the arks produced a hundred or so pounds of fish, not enough to constitute a full-scale revolution but enough to demonstrate beyond question that it is possible to raise food using only sunshine, wind (to operate the pumping system's windmills), and natural biological processes. "We would be raising ninety-five per cent of our food right now if we had time to do enough preserving, canning, and storing," says one of the new alchemists. As it is, their diet consists mainly of their own fish and organically grown fruits and vegetables, occasionally supplemented by milk and cheese from a nearby Stop & Shop. Todd says there is nothing sacrosanct about their diet: in another part of the country it would probably be quite different. "We would have nothing against eating animals if there were plenty of natural grazing land," he says.

The New Alchemy Institute hopes word of its success will get around and inspire others, and indeed, enthusiastic volunteer-workers invariably turn up on weekends. Their newsletter already has some two thousand subscribers. The institute has received a modest amount of foundation support (including some from the Rockefeller Brothers Fund, which, to cover its bets, also supports Green Revolution research), and an offshoot called New Alchemy West is operating in Pescadero, California.

What if we somehow manage to avert the predicted agricultural disaster? Will the alchemists' experiments then have been in vain? On the contrary, if we can begin to wrest ourselves away from conventional food-raising methods and diets—and, just as important, from the conviction that there is such a thing as an innocent bystander—then perhaps something can be done about famine. Those arks on the Cape are at least a beginning. J.F.F.

Hunger and History

Ideas and History

The Way It Was

Art and Archaeology

Letters

Love Stories

SCALA; COVER: BRITISH MUSEUM

The muscular nude on the cover was drawn by Peter Paul Rubens in the early seventeenth century as a copy of Michelangelo's grandly conceived figure at left, painted a century earlier on the ceiling of the Sistine Chapel. Rubens, who looked to Michelangelo as his master, once wrote: "Our feelings are not the same and our techniques are different, but we think in the same large terms. . . ." J. H. Elliott explores Rubens's extraordinary life, his art, and his hugely successful career in an article that begins on page 64.

DRAWING BY JAMES McMULLAN

Money and Revolutions

American, French, Russian, and Chinese revolutionaries all needed cash at one time or another and set about manufacturing some. The printing press, it seems, is deadlier than the guillotine

When the American colonies declared their independence, the 1764 parliamentary ban on paper money became, in a notable modern phrase, inoperative. And however steadily the colonies might have been moving toward more reliable money, there was now no alternative to government paper. It cannot be said that this was an alternative that was embraced with much reluctance. Even before the First Continental Congress assembled, some of the colonies (including Massachusetts) had authorized note issues to pay for military operations. The Congress was without direct powers of taxation; one of its first acts was to authorize a note issue. More states now authorized more notes. And it was by these notes that the American Revolution was financed.

Between June, 1775, and November, 1779, there were forty-two currency issues by the Continental Congress with a total face value of $241,600,000. In the same years the states issued another $209,500,000. Domestic borrowing, much of it rendered in these notes, brought in less than $100,000,000. Reflecting the well-known distaste for such importunity, taxation was insignificant. Taxes levied in consequence of requisitions on the states produced only a few million dollars.

Economics may well be, as Thomas Carlyle wrote, the dismal science, but John Kenneth Galbraith makes it seem otherwise. His latest book, from which this article and the accompanying vignettes are taken, is called *Money: Whence It Came, Where It Went* and will be published this fall by Houghton Mifflin. Like sex, money is generally conceded to be a fine thing but is so beclouded with passion, misunderstanding, and anxiety that it is seldom discussed in the open. We are confident that in Professor Galbraith the whole mythic, agonizing subject has finally found its Freud—or even its Masters and Johnson.

Robert Morris, to whom historians have awarded the less than impeccable title "Financier of the Revolution," obtained some six-and-a-half million dollars in loans from France, a few hundred thousand from Spain, and later, after victory was in prospect, a little over a million from the Dutch. The value of these loans, however, was mainly symbolic. Overwhelmingly, the American Revolution was paid for with paper money.

Since the issues, Continental and state, were far in excess of any corresponding increase in trade, prices rose—at first slowly and then, after 1777, at a rapidly accelerating rate. Congress early took steps to stem the decay, resolving in 1776 that "any person who shall hereafter be so lost to all virtue and regard for his country, as to refuse said bills in payment . . . shall be deemed, published and treated as an enemy in this country and precluded from all trade or intercourse with the inhabitants of these Colonies."

The results, as ever, were disappointing. The price increases continued unchecked. Eventually, in the common saying, "a wagon-load of money would scarcely purchase a wagon-load of provisions." Shoes in Virginia were five thousand dollars a pair in the local notes, a full outfit of clothing more than a million. Creditors sheltered from their debtors like hunted things lest

By JOHN KENNETH GALBRAITH

Galbraith on the History of Money: Not Even Inflation Lasts Forever

It has long been fashionable for historians, except in the secret recesses of their beliefs, to be modest about the lessons of history. Perhaps it teaches only that it teaches little. Where money is concerned, this restraint is unwarranted. The history of money teaches much, or it can be made to teach much. It is, indeed, exceedingly doubtful if much that is durable can be learned about money in any other way. Attitudes toward money proceed in long cyclical swings. When money is bad, people want it to be better. When it is good, they think of other things. Only as matters are examined over time can we see how people who are experiencing inflation yearn for stable money and how those who are accepting the discipline and the costs of stability come to accept the risks of inflation. It is this cycle that teaches us that nothing, not even inflation, is permanent. We learn also that the fear of inflation which inflation leaves in its wake can be as damaging as the inflation itself. From the history we can also see how money and the techniques for its management and mismanagement were evolved and how they now serve or fail to serve. It is from the past that we see how new institutions—corporations, trade unions, the welfare state—have altered the problem of maintaining price stability in the present, and how changing circumstances—movement to a class structure in which fewer and fewer people are successfully taught to take less; the changing political interest of the affluent—have greatly complicated the task.

they be paid off in the worthless notes. As David Ramsey wrote in 1791:

> The widow who lived comfortably on the bequest of a deceased husband, experienced a frustration of all his well-meant tenderness. The laws of the country interposed, and compelled her to receive a shilling where a pound was due. The blooming virgin who had grown up with an unquestionable title to a liberal patrimony was legally stripped of everything but her personal charms and virtues. . . . The dreams of the golden age were realized to the poor man and the debtor, but unfortunately what these gained was just so much taken from others.

The phrase "not worth a Continental" won its enduring place in the American language. Even Benjamin Franklin became ironical: "This Currency, as we manage it, is a wonderful machine. It performs its Office when we issue it; it pays and clothes Troops, and provides Victuals and Ammunition; and when we are obliged to issue a Quantity excessive, it pays itself off by Depreciation."

Thus the United States came into existence on a full tide not of inflation but of hyperinflation—the kind of inflation that ends only in worthless money. What is certain, however, is the absence of any alternative. Taxes, had they been levied by willing legislators on willing people, would have been hard, perhaps impossible, to collect in a country of scattered population, no central government, not the slightest experience in fiscal matters, no tax-collection machinery, and with its coasts and numerous of its ports and customs houses under enemy control.

And people were far from willing. Taxes were disliked for their own sake and also identified with foreign oppression. A rigorous pay-as-you-go policy on the part of the Continental Congress and the states might well have caused the summer patriots (like the monetary conservatives) to have second thoughts about the advantages of independence. Nor was borrowing an alternative. Men of property, then the only domestic source, had no reason to consider the new country a good risk. The loans from France and Spain were motivated not by hope of return but by malice toward an ancient enemy. So only the notes remained. By any rational calculation, it was the paper money that saved the day. Beside the Liberty Bell there might well be a tasteful replica of a Continental note.

It was not a thought to which later historians were attracted. The most influential ones were men for whom hard money and the gold standard were matters not of economics but of morality. The exigent needs of the new country were secondary to what was right. Nor could truth or an eclectic view of the problem faced by the new government be allowed to corrupt or mislead later students or politicians. The monetary experience of the Continental Congress, wrote Davis Rich Dewey in 1903, "has furnished the stock example to nearly every writer on the subject of money. No criticism has been too severe." And Professor Charles J. Bullock concluded, in 1900, that "the opposition which the revolutionary movement encountered from many of the most intelligent and respectable persons in America" was a strong and honest response to their fear, wholly justified by the events, of a reckless use of paper money. To prevent such abuse, one concludes, it would have been worthwhile keeping the British.

Nor have all later scholars relented. A widely read economic history textbook of the post-World War II years concedes that "it is sometimes urged that, since the [Continental] government was weak and the people hated taxes, paper money was the best device available and therefore justifiable." But, the author responds, "To accept such reasoning is to assume an attitude toward economic problems that is fatalistic and subversive of social progress."

In the past century few things more consistently troubled the conservative mind than the fear of paper money. No doubt this was primarily a matter of pecuniary interest—the fear of the creditor that he would be paid off in money of inferior purchasing power, the preference of the merchant for a widely acceptable coin, the ability of the man of means to look at his pile and to know that it would persist, that he would not need a strategy for its preservation. But in the minds of some conservatives there must also have been a lingering sense of the singular service that paper money had, in the recent past, rendered to revolution. Not only was the American Revolution financed with it. So too was the socially far more therapeutic eruption in France. If the French citizens had been required to act within the canons of conventional finance, they could not, any more than the Americans, have acted at all. If paper had served revolutionaries before, might it not do so again—as in Russia after 1917 and in China after World War II?

We have here an explanation of why the revolutionary role of paper money is so little celebrated. The American Revolution would immediately, and the French Revolution would eventually, acquire great respectability. School books would tell schoolchildren of their wonders. But a line had to be drawn. It could not, either in decency or safety, be conceded that anything so wonderful was accomplished by anything so questionable as the Continental notes of the American Revolution or the assignats of the French Revolution.

As might be expected, the design by which the French brought paper to the support of revolution was, in all respects, more subtle, ingenious, and logical than that of the Americans. Indeed, the principle was so plausible that there is a sense of disappointment in the discovery that the result was imperfect. But if the experience was flawed, the end was still served. As Seymour E. Harris has written, "Expediency demanded paper money; the success of the people's Revolution was impossible without it." In order to appreciate the assignats, a prefatory word is essential.

There is very little in economics that invokes the supernatural. But by one phenomenon many have been tempted. In looking at a rectangular piece of paper, on frequent occasion of indifferent quality, featuring a national hero or monument or carrying a classical design with overtones of Peter Paul Rubens, Jacques Louis David, or a particularly well-stocked vegetable market and printed in green or brown ink, they have been assailed by the question: Why is anything intrinsically so valueless so obviously desirable? What, in contrast to a similar mass of fibers clipped from yesterday's newspaper, gives it the power to command goods, enlist service, induce cupidity, promote avarice, invite crime? Surely some magic is involved; certainly some metaphysical or extraterrestrial explanation of its value is required. People who make a profession of knowing about money tend to acquire a priestly reputation. Partly it is because such people are thought to know why valueless paper has value.

The explanation is wholly secular; nor is magic involved. Writers on money have regularly distinguished between three types of currency: (1) that which owes its value, as does gold or silver, to an inherent desirability derived from well-established service to pride of possession, prestige of ownership, personal adornment, dinner plates, or dentistry; (2) that which can readily be exchanged for something of such inherent desirability or which carries the promise, like the early Massachusetts Bay notes, of eventual exchange; and (3) that which is intrinsically worthless, carries no promise that it will be redeemed in anything useful or desirable, and is sustained, at most, by the fiat of the state.

In fact, all three versions are variations on a single theme. John Stuart Mill made the value of money dependent on its supply in relation to the supply of things available for purchase. Were the money gold or silver, there was little chance, the plethora of San Luis Potosí and Sutter's Mill apart, for the amount to increase unduly. This inherent limit on supply was the security that, as money, it would be limited in amount and so retain its value. The same assurance of limited supply held for paper money that was fully convertible into gold and silver. And it held for paper that could not be converted into anything for so long as the supply of such paper was limited. It was the fact of scarcity, not the fact of intrinsic worthlessness, that was important.

. . . on the Gilded Age: When a Dollar Really Was One

There can never have been a time when it was as good to be rich as in the late years of the past century and the first decade of the present one. There was no income tax, and there was the rewarding contrast with the vast majority which was still very poor. Writing in 1899, Thorstein Veblen observed that property was then "the most easily recognized evidence of a reputable degree of success as distinguished from heroic or signal achievement. It therefore becomes the conventional basis of esteem." With sound instinct, historians refer to these years as the Gilded Age.

They might as accurately be called the Age of Gold. For some, and perhaps much, of the esteem ascribed by Veblen to wealth was given by the nature of the money. If money is weak and wasting in value, even the rich lack something in certainty as to their worth. Their minds, like those of others, leap forward to the day when their money will have disintegrated, as did the Continental notes or the Reichsmark. They have a strategy for protecting themselves, but maybe it will not work, and for what then does money count? No such question arises in the minds of its possessor, or of his denigrators, if money is hard and eternal.

In 1900 prices had been generally falling since the end of the Civil War. The prices of wheat, cotton, and other stables were lower by a half as compared with a hundred years earlier. Men of substance could reasonably expect to gain in wealth not only from accumulation of money but from a continuing increase in the purchasing power of what they had.

There were, for the affluent, other agreeable features of the time. Many enjoyments were exclusively the prerogative of the rich, and others did not aspire to them. One such enjoyment was travel. Only the rich went to Europe; the proletariat essayed one westward passage across the Atlantic to America, and that, given the grim amenities of such movement, was more than enough. As no passport was needed unless one ventured into the dubious precincts of the sultan or the czar, so no one needed to worry about rates of exchange. The number of pounds, shillings, and pence that could be had with a hundred dollars was as invariant as the rate at which both currencies could be exchanged into gold. Tariffs apart, there was a similar uniformity in the prices of stable products when converted into pounds, francs, or dollars. In the days before wireless, signal flags at Land's End or other first landfalls told grain ships from the St. Lawrence to proceed to the Thames, Rotterdam, Antwerp, or Hamburg in accordance with fractional advantages in the price in one port or another. Nothing now envisaged for the Common Market comes close to approaching the single and universal monetary system that then existed.

The problem of paper was that, in the absence of convertibility, there was nothing to restrict its supply. Thus it was vulnerable to the unlimited increase that would diminish or destroy its value. The worthlessness of the paper is a detail. Rock quarried at random from the earth's surface and divided into units of a pound and upward would not serve very happily as currency. So great would be the potential supply that the weight of rock for even a minor transaction would be a burden. But rock quarried on the moon and moved to the earth, divided, and with the chunks duly certified as to weight and source, though geologically indistinguishable from the earthbound substance, would be a distinct possibility, at least for as long as the trips were few and the moon rocks retained the requisite scarcity.

The ingenuity of the assignats lay in the commodity into which they could be exchanged and which by its scarcity gave them value. It was not gold and silver; these were not available in sufficient quantity, for, as might be expected, they were principally possessed by those at whom the Revolution was directed. Thus they had been secreted or sent or taken abroad. The supporting and restricting asset was land, the very thing that the Revolution was making available—which, in large measure, the Revolution was all about. Land could not be hidden. And not even the most ingenious émigré could take it with him. It was also something that could not be increased in total amount. For this reason it was something that those who remained in France were as pleased to possess as gold itself.

The initial resource was the land not of the aristocracy but of the Church. This is usually estimated to have amounted to a fifth of all the land in France in 1789. The Estates-General had been summoned in consequence of the terrible fiscal straits of the realm. No more could be borrowed. There was no central bank that could be commanded to take up loans. All still depended on the existence of willing lenders or those who could be apprehended and impressed with their duty. The Third Estate could scarcely be expected to vote new or heavier levies when its members were principally concerned with the regressive harshness of those then being collected. In fact, on June 17, 1789, the National Assembly declared all taxes illegal, a breathtaking step softened by the provision that they might be collected on a temporary basis. Meanwhile, memories of John Law* kept Frenchmen acutely suspicious of ordinary paper money; during 1788, a proposal for an interest-bearing note issue provoked so much opposition that it had to be withdrawn. But a note issue that could be redeemed in actual land was something different. The clerical lands were an endowment by Heaven of the Revolution.

The decisive action was taken on December 19, 1789. An issue of 400 million livres was authorized; they would, it was promised, "pay off the public debt, animate agriculture and industry and have the lands better administered." These notes, the assignats, were to be redeemed within five years from the sale of an equivalent value of the lands of the Church and the Crown. The first assignats bore interest at 5 per cent; anyone with an appropriate amount could use them directly in exchange for land. In the following summer, when a new large issue was authorized, the interest was eliminated. Later still, small denominations were issued.

*Law's financial schemes, including wholesale printing of paper money, culminated disastrously in 1720. See "The Scoundrel Who Invented Credit," Spring, 1971

There were misgivings. The memory of Law continued to be invoked. An anonymous American intervened with *Advice on the Assignats by a Citizen of the United States*. He warned the Assembly against the assignats out of the recent rich experience of his own country with Continental notes. However, the initial response to the land-based currency was generally favorable.

Had it been possible to stop with the original issue or that of 1790, the assignats would be celebrated as a remarkably interesting innovation. Here was not a gold, silver, or tobacco standard, but one based solidly and logically on the good soil of France. Purchasing power in the first years had stood up well. There was admiring talk of how the assignats had put land into circulation. And business had improved, employment had increased, and sales of Church and other public lands had been facilitated. On occasion, sales had been too good. In relation to annual income, the prices set were comparatively modest; speculators clutching large packages of

. . . on Nomenclature: The Cosmetic Noun from 1907 to 1974

Where economic misfortune is concerned, a word on nomenclature is necessary. In the course of his disastrous odyssey, Pal Joey, the most inspired of John O'Hara's creations, finds himself singing in a cheap Chicago nightclub strictly for cakes and coffee. He explains this misfortune by saying that the *panic* is still on. His term—archaic and thus slightly pretentious—reflects the unfailing O'Hara ear. During the past century, and until 1907, the United States had panics, and that, unabashedly, is what they were called. But by 1907 language was becoming, like so much else, the servant of economic interest. To minimize the shock, businessmen and bankers had started to explain that any economic setback was not a panic, only a crisis. They were undeterred by the use of this term in a more ominous context—that of the ultimate capitalist crisis—by Marx. By the 1920's, however, the word "crisis" had also acquired a fearsome connotation. Accordingly, men offered reassurance by explaining that it was not a crisis, only a depression. A very soft word. Then the Great Depression associated the most frightful of economic misfortunes with that term, and economic semanticists now explained that no depression was in prospect, at most only a recession. In the 1950's, when there was a modest setback, economists and public officials were united in denying that it was a recession—only a sidewise movement or a rolling readjustment. Herbert Stein, the amiable man whose difficult honor it was to serve as the economic voice of Richard Nixon, would have referred to the panic of 1893 as a growth correction.

. . . on the Rhetoric of Hard Times: Telling It Like It Isn't

In the summer of 1819, fifty thousand workers were thought to be unemployed in New York, Philadelphia, and Baltimore. In Poughkeepsie an ingenious and self-reliant toiler named John Daely pleaded guilty to stealing a horse, explaining that "he could get no work, and could hit upon no other plan so ready and certain to provide him with a home and steady employment." His plan succeeded; he was given eight years. A newspaper, surveying the situation, thought that "a deeper gloom hangs over us than was ever witnessed by the oldest man. The last war was sunshine compared with these times." Eighteen years later, after the panic of 1837, the New York *Herald* concluded that "the United States were never in such a perilous condition as they are at this moment." In a burst of chivalrous compassion, it went on to say that "we weep and mourn for the poor, blushing, weeping, defenseless, innocent, beauteous females who are involved in the general crash." Every later panic brought similar expressions of despair and almost equally alarming prose.

The panics also brought recourse to a line of remedial action that has always been favored. This is to seek to exorcise economic misfortune by affirming that it does not exist. In November, 1820, a very dark month following the crash of the year before, James Monroe advised the Congress of the "prosperous and happy" condition of the country, adding that "it is impossible to behold so gratifying, so glorious a spectacle, without being penetrated with the most profound and grateful acknowledgments to the Supreme Author of All Good for such manifold and inestimable blessings." The government at the time was known to be deeply concerned over the economic crisis. In March, 1837, as the trials of that terrible year were becoming felt, Andrew Jackson said in his farewell address: "I leave this great people prosperous and happy." In June, 1930, Herbert Hoover was visited by a delegation of public-spirited men who urged an expansion of public works to ease the plight of the unemployed who were then rising into the millions. "Gentlemen," the president said, "you have come sixty days too late. The depression is over." In the sincerity of manner with which they endlessly proclaimed the end of inflation, Richard Nixon and his economists were acting in a tradition older than they knew.

the assignats had arrived to take advantage of the bargains.

However, in France, as in America earlier, the demands of revolution were insistent. Although the land was limited, the claims upon it could be increased. The large issue of 1790 was followed by others—especially after war broke out in 1792. Prices denominated in assignats now rose; their rate of exchange for gold and silver, dealing in which had been authorized by the Assembly, declined sharply. In 1793 and 1794, under the Convention and the management of Joseph Cambon, there was a period of stability. Prices were fixed with some success. What could have been more important, the supply of assignats was curtailed by the righteous device of repudiating those that had been issued under the king. In these years they retained a value of around 50 per cent of their face amount when exchanged for gold or silver.

Soon, however, need again asserted itself. More and more were printed. In an innovative step in economic warfare, William Pitt, after 1793, allowed the Royalist émigrés to manufacture assignats for export to France. This, it was hoped, would hasten the decay. In the end, the French presses were printing one day to supply the needs of the next. Soon the Directory halted the exchange of good real estate for the now nearly worthless paper—France went off the land standard. Creditors were also protected from having their debts paid in assignats. This saved them from the ignominy of having to hide from their debtors. A new paper currency, the *mandats territoriaux*, also carrying an entitlement to land, met, not surprisingly, with an adverse response. In February, 1797, the Directory returned to gold and silver. But by then the Revolution was an accomplished fact. It had been financed by the assignats. They have at least as good a claim on memory as the guillotine.

Paper was similarly to serve the Soviets in and after the Russian Revolution. By 1920 around 85 per cent of the state budget was being met by the manufacture of paper money. In that year, or not long after, a Harvard graduate student in economics visited the Soviet Union. In accordance with the counsel of similar adventurers of the time he took in his pocket a wad of toilet paper. On a densely crowded streetcar in Moscow one day he felt the hand of a thief in his hip pocket. He noted with amusement and satisfaction that it was the pocket that contained not his rubles but the toilet paper. Only later did the young scholar come to realize that the product that was stolen was more valuable than the packet of notes in the other pocket. In the aftermath of the Revolution the Soviet Union, like the other Communist states, became a stern defender of stable prices and hard money. But the Russians, like the Americans and the French, owe their revolution to paper money.

Not that the use of paper is a guarantee of revolutionary success. In 1913 in the old Spanish town of Chihuahua, Pancho Villa was carrying out his engaging combination of banditry and social reform. Soldiers were cleaning the streets, land was being given to the peons, children were being put in schools, and Villa was printing money by the square yard. This money could not be exchanged for any better asset. It promised nothing. It was sustained by no residue of prestige or esteem. It was abundant. Its only claim to worth was Pancho Villa's signature. He gave this money to whosoever seemed to be in need or anyone who struck his fancy. It did not bring him success, although he did enjoy a measure of popularity while it lasted. But the United States Army pursued him; more orderly men intervened to persuade him to retire to a hacienda in Durango. There, a decade later, when he was suspected by some to be contemplating another foray into banditry, social reform, and monetary policy, he was assassinated.

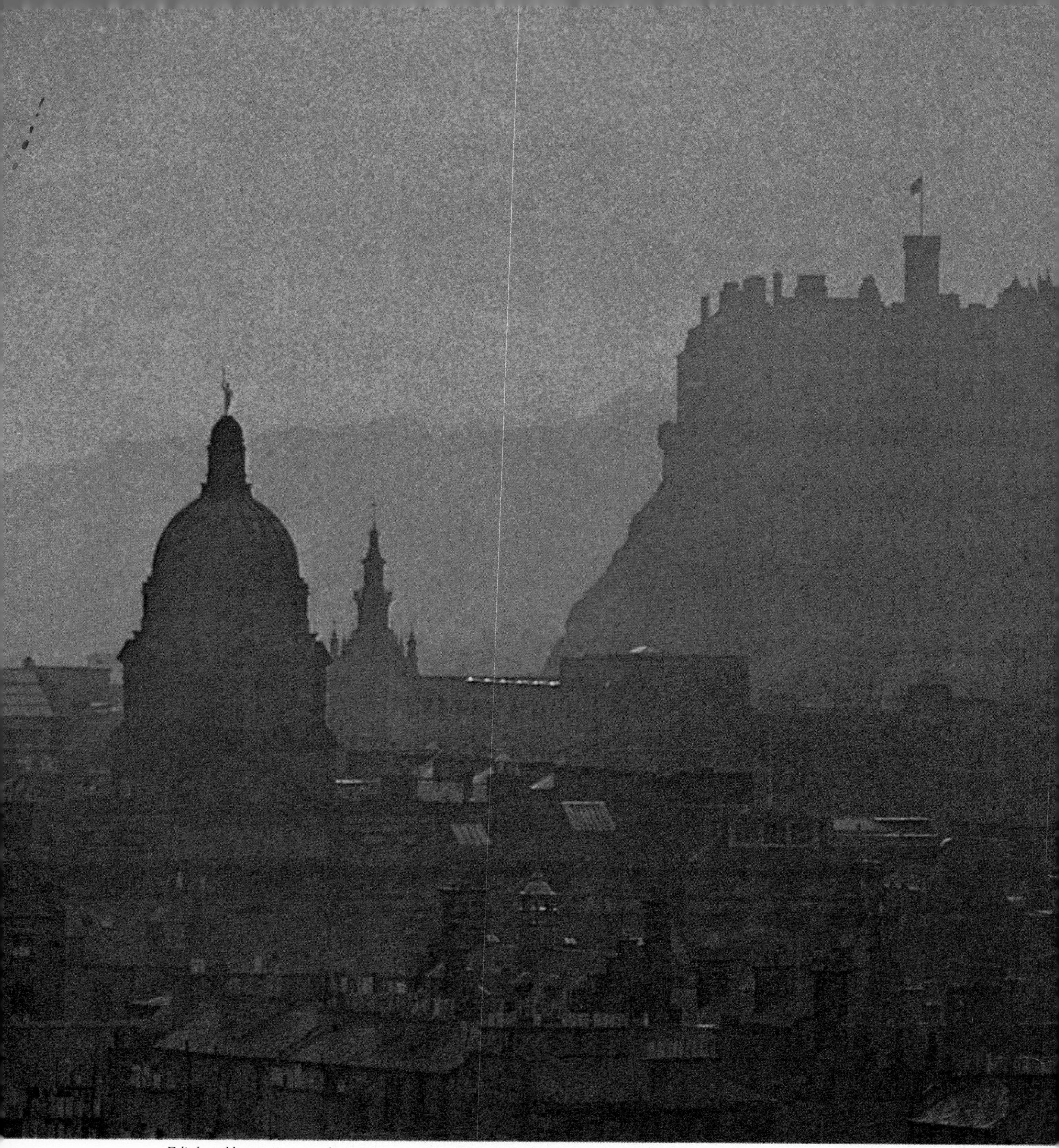

Edinburgh's ancient castle, atop a 400-foot-high cliff, dominates the city's crowded Old Town. The tall spire at right is Assembly Ha

The Golden Age of Edinburgh

the left is the dome of Edinburgh University's Old Quadrangle, topped by a figure of Youth holding aloft the torch of knowledge.

In the late eighteenth century, a Scottish town without wealth or size or power became pre-eminent among the great cities of Europe. Who turned Edinburgh into the "Athens of the North"?

By WALTER KARP

PHOTOGRAPHED FOR HORIZON BY SONJA BULLATY AND ANGELO LOMEO

The Rational City

SCOTTISH NATIONAL PORTRAIT GALLERY

James Craig

In 1767, when his plan for Edinburgh's New Town was approved, James Craig was an unknown young architect. Overnight he achieved fame, for his design was a masterpiece of rational planning—both a reflection and a harbinger of the Enlightenment ideals then gathering force. Craig died in 1795, before construction was completed, but New Town in all its glory differed only slightly from his original plan. It was a fitting part of the "Athens of the North."

In March, 1766, the town council of Edinburgh offered a gold medal for the "best plan of a New Town" to be constructed to the north of the city. The idea was eminently practical: if Edinburgh needed anything, it needed new housing, for no city in the world was more densely populated, its inhabitants living chiefly in apartment houses, some as many as twelve stories high. The members of the council, however, had much more in mind than mere housing. They intended to create a new city dedicated to elegance, refinement, and learning, a capital of enlightened thought and classical ideals. And the remarkable thing is that they almost succeeded. In the annals of cities there is nothing to match the transformation of Edinburgh—a city blessed with neither wealth nor size nor power—into one of the pre-eminent cultural and intellectual centers of Europe, "The Athens of the North."

In 1766 Edinburgh most emphatically did not look or feel (or smell) like a center of enlightened thought and classical ideals. Until only a few years before, it had seethed with dark royal conspiracies and fierce theological disputes, centuries apart in spirit from the European Age of Reason. Physically, it was peculiarly grim and gothic. At the city's west end stood a brooding medieval castle, squatting atop an awesome four-hundred-foot pile of rocks. A mile away, at the east end, stood the bloodstained Palace of Holyroodhouse, linked to the castle by a ridge along which ran the city's High Street with its gloomy tenements. Built as far back as the sixteenth century, Edinburgh's unique apartment houses compressed between them a dark maze of sloping alleys and courtyards as dreary as dungeons and noxiously smelly.

The chief amusements were the city's uncomfortable, dimly lit tav-

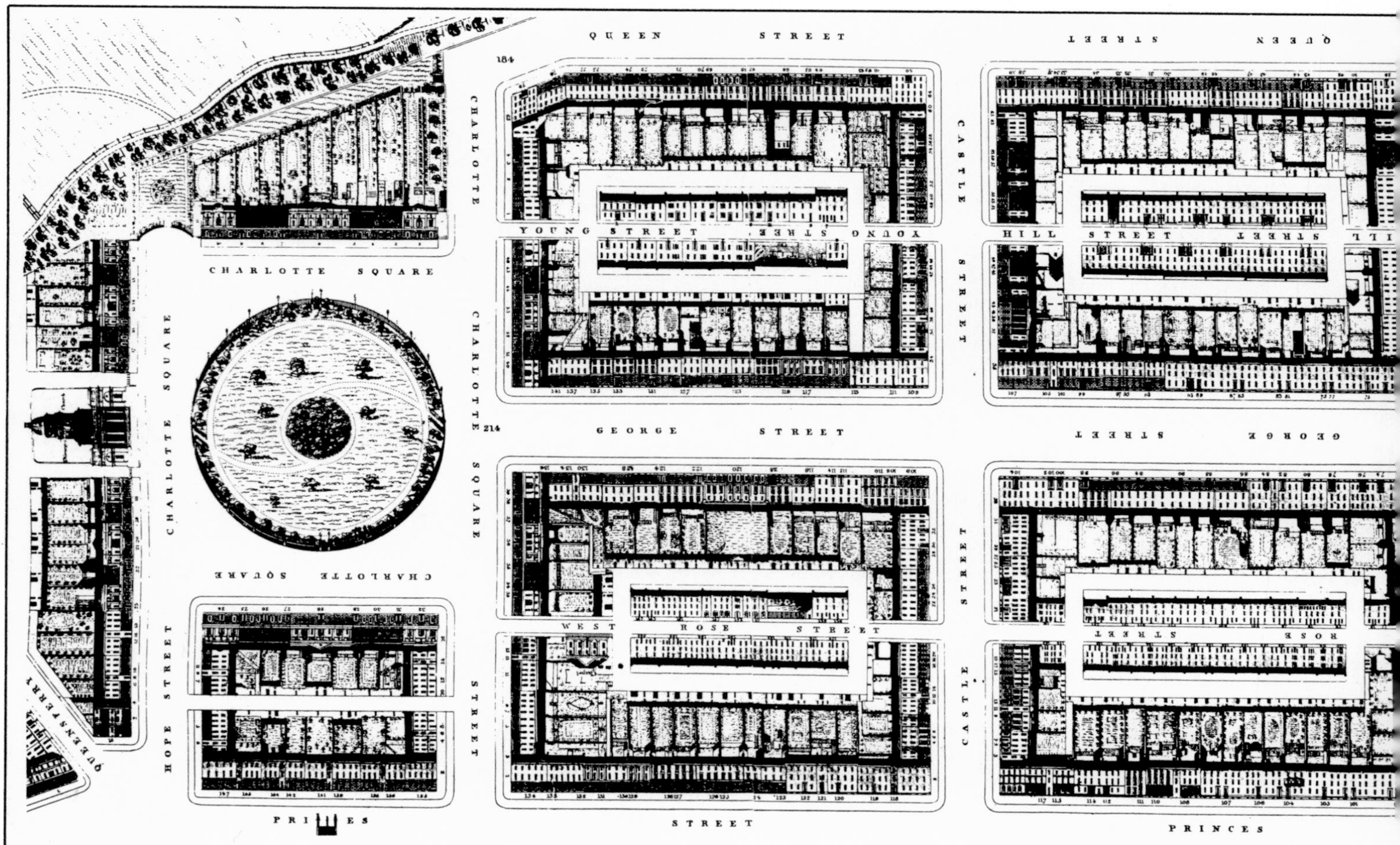

New Town, 1819: In Craig's plan, all houses faced major thoroughfares, and most had large gardens in the rear.

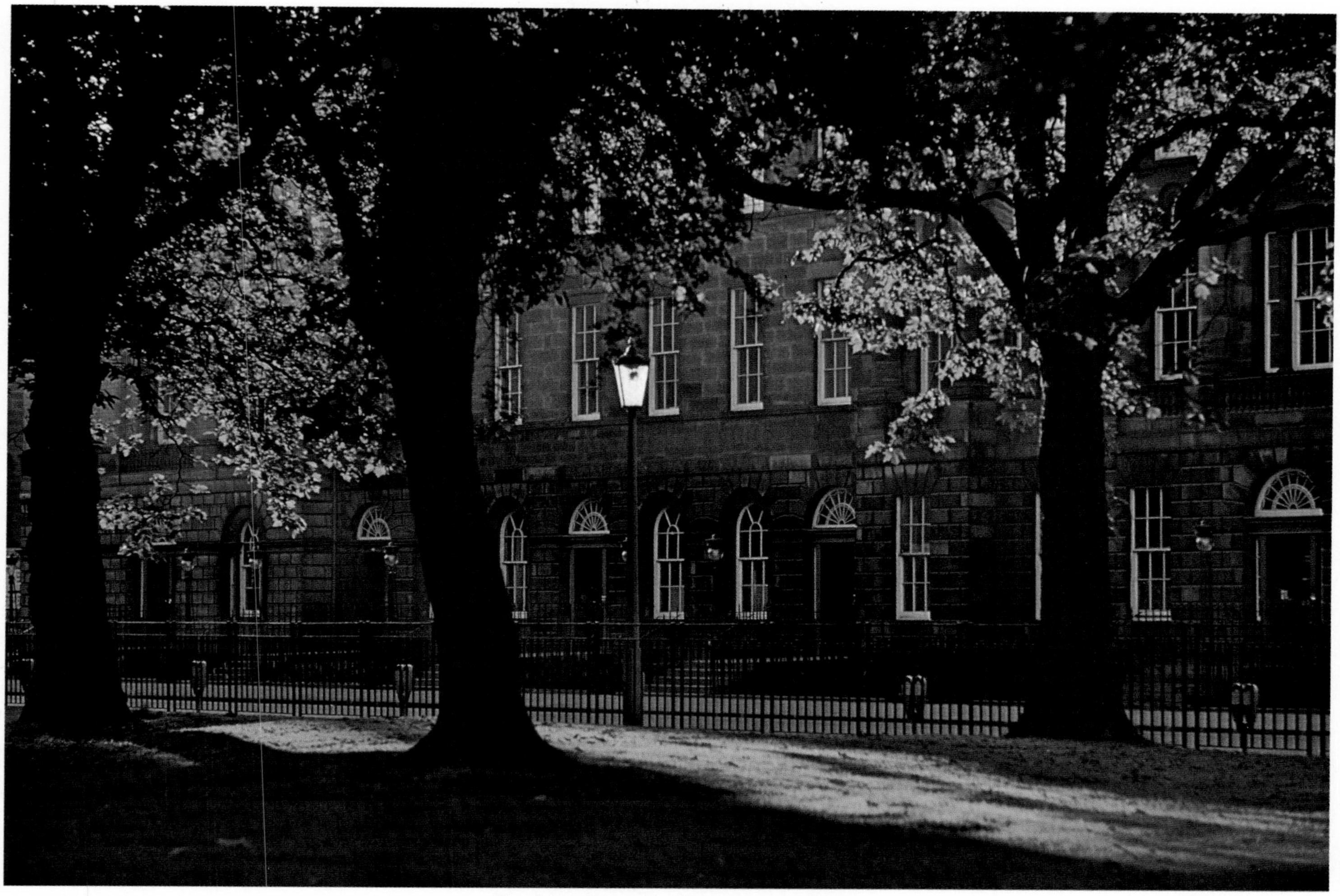

Charlotte Square in the autumn sunlight

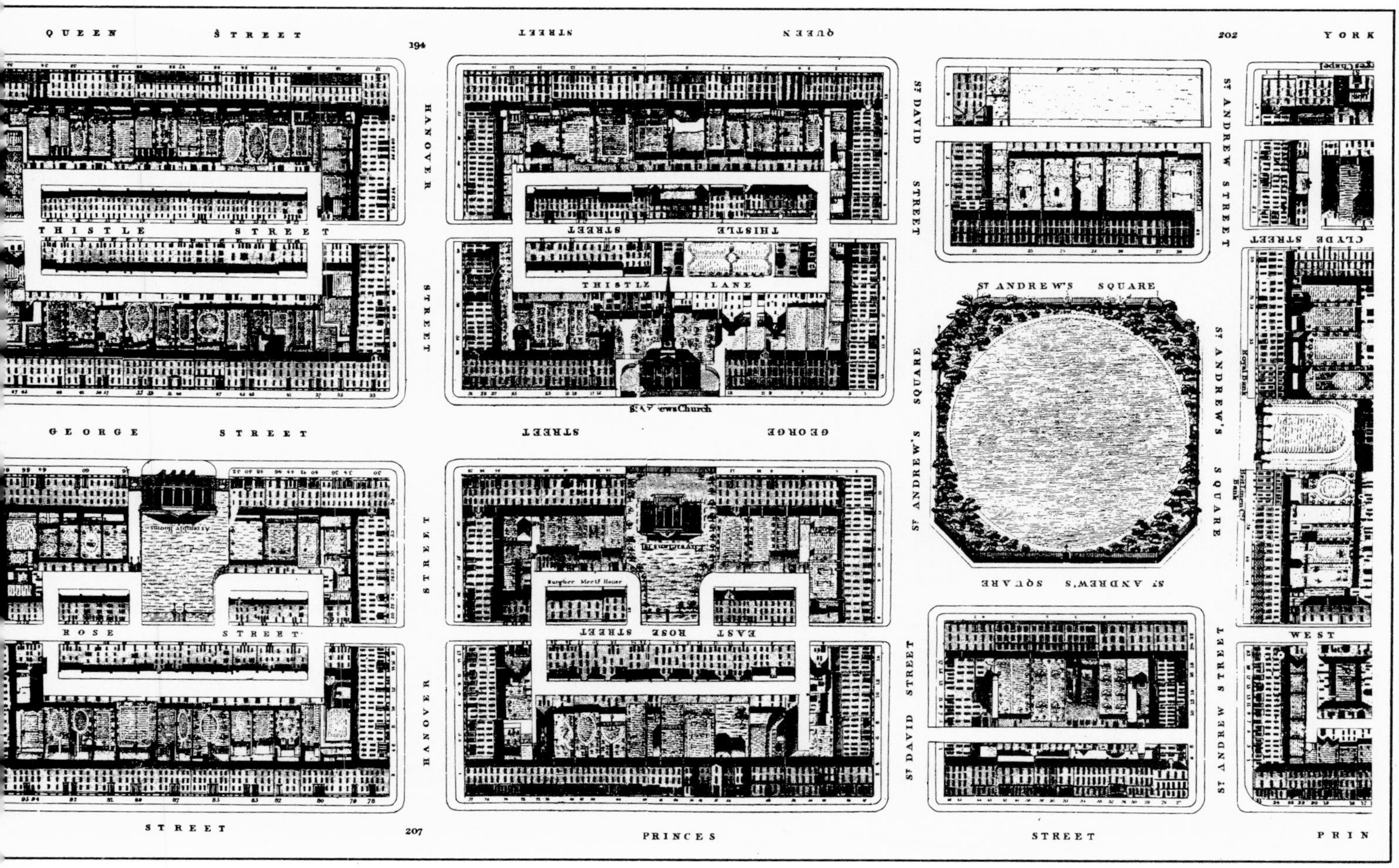

UNIVERSITY LIBRARY, EDINBURGH

"Auld Reekie"

UNIVERSITY LIBRARY, EDINBURGH

"Rag-fair" in St. Mary's Wynd, Old Town

Edinburgh's golden age began in the smoky reaches of Old Town, where the fumes rising from a myriad of chimneys gave the city its nickname. The progenitor of that age was Allan Ramsay, a wigmaker turned bookseller and poet, who died in 1775, long before the New Town was even proposed. Ramsay was the first true vernacular bard of Scotland, using the language of the Scots to celebrate the life of the common folk—the men and women who roamed the wynds and closes of Old Town and the shepherds and peasants of the outlying hills and fields. He also organized the first circulating library in Scotland, and founded the Easy Club in emulation of London's Queen Anne Wits. Though little known—and rarely read—today, Ramsay, by his poetry and his spirited defense of secular literature, paved the way for the golden age to follow.

Allan Ramsay

erns, and when an Edinburgh man went to a tavern he expected to return home drunk. Edinburgh in the Age of Reason was a city of sots. As a native son recalled years later, deep drinking in the taverns "prevailed in Edinburgh to an incredible extent, and engrossed the leisure hours of all professional men, scarcely excepting even the most stern and dignified. . . . Nothing was so common in the morning, as to meet a nobleman or two reeling home from a close in the High Street, where they had spent the whole night in drinking. Nor was it unusual to find the half of his Majesty's most honourable Lords of Council and Session mounting the Bench, in the forenoon, in a state little removed from absolute civilation."

For all its Calvinist upbringing, the city was a remarkably raucous place. An Englishman named Edward Topham, visiting there in 1774–75, was amazed to discover that the "shrine of festivities" for the "First People of Edinburgh" was none other than an oysterhouse where men and women gathered round a vast table, stuffed themselves with oysters, drank potsful of porter, and then crowned the evening dancing hectic reels. The music would commence, observed Topham, and up the ladies would "start, animated with new life, and you would imagine they had received an electrical shock, or been bit by a tarantula." The people of Edinburgh, he noted, "are exceedingly fond of jovial company." Since aristocrats, lawyers, and tailors still lived together in the same apartment houses (the affluent taking the middle floors), they were none too fussy about the mingling of classes. One of Edinburgh's innumerable lawyers, James Boswell, once warned Rousseau, of all people, about the "shocking familiarity" of Scotsmen—that is, their woeful disrespect for the distinctions of rank.

Above all, there was a general harshness in the mores and manners of the city. It could be seen in the much-detested City Guard, a band of fierce Highlanders who used battle-axes to overawe the citizenry. It was visible in the city jail, the Old Tolbooth, which stood in the middle of the High Street until 1817, its nickname, the "heart of Midlothian," a harsh jest about Scots harshness. Even dancing, one of Edinburgh's favorite pastimes, came under an exacting, if comical regimen. Throughout the eighteenth century, dance-going youths had to suffer the petty despotism of "Lady Directresses" who assigned dancing partners by a system of numbered tickets, apparently to prevent anyone from dancing with someone he liked. "Woe on the poor girl," an Edinburgh man recalled, "who with ticket 2.7, was found opposite a youth marked 5.9! It was flirting without a licence, and looked very ill." Yet the opening of Edinburgh's first public dancing place, the Old Assembly Room, was hailed as a "symptom of the gradual softening away of the sombre habits of the people."

Clearly, one reason Edinburgh found elegance and refinement so attractive was that there was so little of either when the city's golden age commenced. Yet for all that, Edinburgh was already a major intellectual center when Topham was trying to convince his fellow Englishmen that the detested Scots were worth their "attention." In the year of his visit, there sat at the pinnacle of Edinburgh society the most penetrating, the most celebrated, the most controversial philosopher in Europe, none other than the great David Hume, who had returned from Paris to his native city in 1769 and found it so much to his liking he was resolved never to leave. Soon to settle down in Edinburgh, too, was Hume's good friend Adam Smith, then completing *The Wealth of Nations* but already

The Grassmarket, a square in Old Town, with the castle in the backgrou

GRASSMARK
GENTLEMEN

famous in Europe for demonstrating in his *Theory of Moral Sentiments* one of the fundamental tenets of Edinburgh thought, that men were born with an innate moral sense.

Gathered around Hume were such luminaries as William Robertson, widely regarded as one of the greatest historians of the time; Adam Ferguson, the political philosopher (Dr. Johnson said to him, "Sir, I perceive you are a vile Whig," when Boswell introduced them in 1772); Joseph Black, one of the great figures in the history of chemistry as well as professor of medicine and chemistry at the university; the brothers Adam, the great neoclassical architects (though Robert, as architect to George III, lived principally in London). Around the major lights were a bevy of pioneer physicians, surgeons, and historians, as well as literary men such as Henry Mackenzie, author of *The Man of Feeling*, an early novel of sensibility, and, like so many Edinburgh savants, a practicing lawyer. There was also the eccentric Lord Monboddo, another eminent Edinburgh jurist, and in many ways a representative Edinburgh savant, what with his learned researches into the origins of language and his fondness for giving supper parties aimed at reviving the manners and style of antiquity.

But Edinburgh also had much more. Back of these major thinkers and scholars, supporting them, was an entire society in love with learning. Edinburgh was a city whose social leaders aspired to be savants, or at the very least the friend of savants—no difficult task, for everybody knew everybody else in the city. (The population as late as 1800 was a mere 67,000.) Lovers of learning could meet each other by strolling along the High Street, the city's agora, between one and two P.M. Or they could drop in on each other's supper parties, say their "good e'ens," and stay for oysters, ale, and good talk. Or they could join each other's social clubs, of which there were dozens in the city, including the Poker Club, to which both Smith and Hume belonged.

It was a society that relished, to a remarkable degree, high-flown abstract discussions. As the Reverend Sydney Smith, a celebrated English wit, once said, he spent five years in Edinburgh "discussing metaphysics and medicine in that garret of the earth." The people, he said, "are so imbued with metaphysics that they even make love metaphysically. I overheard a young lady of my acquaintance, at a dance in Edinburgh, exclaim, in a sudden pause of the music, 'What you say, my Lord, is very true of love in the *aibstract*, but'—here the fiddlers began fiddling furiously, and the rest was lost." Smith was not exaggerating. An amorous Edinburgh lady once tried to ensnare Robert Burns by insisting that she and the young poet were kindred in their feelings, "tho' the pen of a Locke could not define them," which is assuredly the metaphysics of temptation.

It was a testament to Edinburgh's love of learning that Adam Smith was a leading Edinburgh host, a role he would have been singularly unfit to play outside Edinburgh. Not only was Smith extremely absent-minded. He was also wont to sit sunk in thought in the midst of social gatherings and then burst into full-blown lectures on whatever happened to be in his mind. Once, while delivering a stern critique of a leading politician, Smith suddenly realized that the man's closest relative was at the table. "Deil care, Deil care," he muttered. "It's all true."

It was a testament, too, to the municipal love of learning that the town council, exercising its ancient right to appoint professors to the university, chose eminently deserving men. In the atmosphere of Edinburgh,

MARY EVANS PICTURE LIBRARY

Carousers in a tavern, circa 1773

"Every gentleman a drunkard and every drunkard a gentleman"

Or, the habits and hangovers of Enlightened Edinburgh

A quiet pub on the High Street

In eighteenth-century Edinburgh, temperance was an unknown virtue. As the historian Henry Grey Graham wrote, "It was a convivial age, and it was a drinking society."

To be sure, the inhabitants of Edinburgh probably felt they had good reason to imbibe. They had but recently broken free from a stifling Calvinistic authority that, to quote Graham again, "uttered anathemas against all worldly pleasure." Then, too, there were the dreadful conditions in Old Town. The tenements, though picturesque, were often poorly built and usually poorly maintained. They could also be dangerous. Parliament tried to limit new buildings to a height of five stories. The law applied, however, only to the front section of a building, and in hilly Edinburgh this often produced tenements with the permissible five stories in the front

Boswell in full gear

and, as a nineteenth-century author observed, "eight, ten, or even more floors" in the back. However, he went on to say, "it is generally understood, that if a house falls, it cannot be rebuilt of the same height."

In such a community, where families shared cramped quarters and mutual stairways, the only refuge was the taverns—for both business and pleasure. But "the transaction of business," says Graham, "was more the excuse than the reason for attendance." He also described a businessman's typical day: "When St. Giles' bells played out half-past eleven in the morning each citizen went to get a gill of ale, which was known as his 'meridian,' although before breakfast he had paid a similar visit, and in the course of the day he went not seldom with his customers to drink over their bargains. . . . In the evenings citizens were back at their familiar haunt to spend the evening with congenial friends over a simple fare, with ale or claret, till the town guard beat the ten o'clock drum, warning all decent burghers to withdraw soberly to bed." Despite the warning,

RADIO TIMES HULTON

Dowie's Tavern in Old Town

"the topers sat on, magistrates being the most habitual violators of their own laws, and men drank not merely 'from the gill-bell to the drum,' but long after."

Memoirs of Edinburgh citizens abound with stories of riotous debauch and headachy remorse. Most notable in this respect, perhaps, is James Boswell, whose diaries record innumerable instances of "jovial roaring" and morning-after "squeamishness," often cured with "old hock, which just cooled my fever and really sobered me." Boswell frequently chastised himself for his "hobbing and nobbing," repeatedly vowing to be temperate in the future. But his good intentions were rarely more than that, and he seems to have shared the general Edinburgh attitude that intemperance was, at most, a "venial blemish."

The favored drink of the literati was claret, but whisky was not to be scoffed at. It was even celebrated in song by such poets as Robert Burns, who once declared that "freedom and whisky gang thegither." Burns liked to frequent a narrow room, known as "the coffin," in John Dowie's tavern, drinking with clerks and advocates during the day and men of letters at night. On his deathbed, it is said, Burns exclaimed: "O these Edinburgh gentles [gentlemen]—if it hadna been for them I had a constitution would have stood onything!"

Burns's constitution lasted thirty-seven years. Others were not so lucky. Robert Fergusson, a gifted vernacular poet who extolled the common life of "Auld Reekie," succumbed early. In 1773 he wrote *A Drink Eclogue*, a dialogue between a landlady,

RADIO TIMES HULTON

Robert Fergusson

brandy, and whisky, in which brandy describes itself as a "sweetly gusted cordial dose." A year later, at the age of twenty-four, he was dead.

Unconcerned, the literati continued to patronize the taverns, which also served as meeting places for a variety of clubs, ranging from the Industrious Club and the Pious Club (which convened in a piehouse) to the Sweating Club and the Spendthrift Club (members' expenditures were limited to fivepence an evening). One notable clubman, Henry Dundas, belonged both to the Poker Club, an abstemious group that included David Hume, and to the Wig Club, famous for its consumption of a potent local brew called Twopenny. Its ballot box was in the shape of a naked man, and its seal, according to one prudish historian, "could not nowadays be exhibited in decent society."

The height of conviviality was achieved by the short-lived Right and Wrong Club. One member, James Hogg, described the proceedings in his autobiography: "We dined at five and separated at two in the morning before which time the Club had risen greatly in our estimation; so we agreed to meet the next day and every successive day for five or six weeks, and during all that time our hours of sitting continued the same. . . . The result

NATIONAL PORTRAIT GALLERY, LONDON

Henry Dundas, first Lord Melville

was that several of the members got quite deranged, and I drank myself into an inflamatory fever. . . . They continued their meetings for some days longer . . . and I was sometimes favoured with a call from one or more of the members at two or three in the morning when they separated. The morning after such visits I was almost sure to have to provide new knockers and bell handles for all the people on the stairs."

The Right and Wrong Club was founded—and died—in 1814. By that time, the riotous night life of Edinburgh was over. As gentlemen and men of letters moved to the New Town—or away from the city altogether—social life hardened into genteel formality. And though the health of its citizens no doubt benefited, something vital and alive was lost forever. —K.E.

the council, however "silent, powerful, submissive, mysterious" it was (to quote a contemporary critic), would not have dared to do otherwise. Edinburgh, in short, was a society where the worldly and the learned mixed and mingled easily, with every mark of mutual respect. If the worldly took pleasure in learning, the learned returned the compliment by taking pleasure in worldly society. In this, as in other ways, Hume was the archetypical Edinburgh savant, conjoining as he did an intellect of unsurpassed rigor with the personality of an affable clubman.

Just why a municipality should become so "imbued with metaphysics" is one of the mysteries of cultural history. According to the English essayist Walter Bagehot, writing in 1876, the "educated world in Scotland" flourished by virtue of a fortunate social interregnum. "The Union with England [in 1707] had removed the aristocracy of birth which overshadowed it before, and commerce had not yet created the aristocracy of wealth which overshadows it now. Philosophical merit had therefore then in Scotland an excellent chance of being far better regarded than it usually is in the world. There were educated people who cared for philosophy, and these people had prizes to give away." No doubt more was involved, but Bagehot's explanation is probably as good as any, although it is worth adding that two centuries of disputatious theology had given Scotsmen a taste for speculative thought and that the native respect for any "lad o' pairts" made it easier for the man of humble birth to rise in Edinburgh than in any other city in caste-ridden Europe.

The strengths and weaknesses of Edinburgh's educated world were graphically displayed in the winter of 1786–87, when Scotland's greatest "lad o' pairts," the farmer-poet Robert Burns, came to town to seek his fortune on the strength of some published verses and on the back of a borrowed pony. At once the doors of Edinburgh society were flung open in welcome, and through the doors the twenty-eight-year-old Burns passed in triumph: breakfasts, teas, dinners, suppers, a blaze of weighty admiration and flattering erudite attention. Shriveled old Lord Monboddo invited Burns to one of his Grecian supper parties. Dr. Robertson applauded the vigor of Burns's talk, all the more remarkable in a man who had spent most of his life treading behind a plowhorse. Dr. Hugh Blair, professor of rhetoric and belles-lettres, passed approving judgment on his verse. Adam Ferguson invited him to a party where a fifteen-year-old admirer, Walter Scott, met the lion of the season and came away impressed with the poet's composure among men vastly more learned than he and considerably more polished.

Ten days after arriving in the city, Burns wrote home triumphantly: "I am in a fair way of becoming as eminent as Thomas a Kempis or John Bunyan; and you may expect henceforth to see my birthday inserted among the wonderful events, in the Poor Robin's and Aberdeen Almanacks. . . . My Lord Glencairn and the Dean of Faculty, Mr. H. Erskine have taken me under their wing; and by all probability I shall soon be the tenth Worthy, and the eighth Wise Man of the world."

All this was heady stuff for an impoverished farmer who longed to escape the plow. Yet there was something disquieting about Edinburgh's appreciation of the Rustic Bard. The truth is, what was best in Burns's poems Edinburgh's literati did not much enjoy. Dr. Blair disliked their liberal political leanings; another savant told Burns candidly that he used Scottish dialect too much; the lawyer-novelist Mackenzie, in an article hailing Burns's genius, had to admit that the poet's Muse was

Bewigged advocates take a break at Parliament House

A Legal Turn of Mind

David Hume

The law attracted the most brilliant members of Edinburgh's literati, including that penetrating intellect, David Hume, who for a time was Keeper of the Advocates' Library. The great philosopher-historian was later lionized in Europe and in his own Edinburgh: when he moved in 1772 to an unnamed street, in New Town, a female admirer promptly dubbed it St. David's Street, the name it bears to this day. Although he did not live to see its inception in 1802, Hume would no doubt have applauded the Edinburgh Review, *founded by two young members of the bar, Henry Brougham and Francis Jeffrey, and a clergyman-scholar who always dreamed of being a lawyer, Sydney Smith. Adamantly Whig in its political essays, and often obtuse in its literary judgments, the* Review *nevertheless provided a forum for intelligent criticism and persisted until 1929.*

Henry Brougham

Sydney Smith

Francis Jeffrey

Rustic Bards vs. The Literati

Robert Burns

When Robert Burns came to town in 1786, he was welcomed enthusiastically by Edinburgh's literati, led by Dr. Hugh Blair. The country boy did not altogether please Dr. Blair and his friends: they fretted over his choice of residences, disapproved of his drinking companions, and objected to the crude language and earthy emotion in his poetry. Yet their distrust of his verse is understandable, for a quarter-century earlier, they had unwittingly championed another rustic poet, James Macpherson, whose Fingal*—purportedly a translation of a third-century bard named Ossian—was published in 1761. When, the following year, Dr. Blair wrote a glowing tribute to* The Poems of Ossian, *he thought he was extolling another translation by the ancient Gaelic poet. But* Ossian *was soon branded as a fake, and it was not until the early nineteenth century that the work was acclaimed for what it was—a skillful blend of Highland tradition, Gaelic songs, and Macpherson's poetic talent.*

SCOTTISH ROOM, CENTRAL LIBRARY, EDINBURGH

FINGAL,
AN
ANCIENT EPIC POEM,
In SIX BOOKS:
Together with several other POEMS, composed by
OSSIAN the Son of FINGAL.
Translated from the Galic Language,
By JAMES MACPHERSON.
Fortia facta patrum. VIRGIL.

LONDON:
Printed for T. Becket and P. A. De Hondt, in the Strand.
M DCC LXII.

Title page of Fingal

NATIONAL PORTRAIT GALLERY, LONDON

James Macpherson

"a little unguarded in her ridicule of hypocrisy." What genuinely enthralled the speculative minds of Edinburgh's savants was that Burns had a Muse at all. To the savants he was, as Mackenzie dubbed him, "the heaven-taught ploughman," the living proof of Edinburgh's central tenet that nobility of heart is innate, even in an untutored Scots plowman. To the savants of Edinburgh, Burns was not so much a first-rate poet as he was a first-rate confirmation of their theories.

What was equally disquieting for Burns was the sharply divided life he was leading. By day he stood, often enough, in the drawing rooms of the New Town, and at night he had to return over the thousand-foot-long North Bridge to a mean tenement in the High Street, where the female lodgers on the floor above did not "make love metaphysically." Burns discovered that soon enough. "As our floors are low and ill-plaistered, we can easily distinguish our laughter-loving, night-rejoicing neighbors—when they are eating, when they are drinking, when they are singing, when they are etc." But if the savants of the New Town had their charms for the poet, so did the raucous inhabitants of the Old Town. The savants grew fretful when they learned that their "heaven-taught ploughman" was spending time in the old city's taverns among bawdy-talking, hard-drinking company by no means devoted to elegance, classicism, and noble sentiments. Once, such diversions would scarcely have mattered, but Edinburgh was fast becoming a divided city and the New Town itself had accelerated the process.

In July, 1767, the Town Council had approved a town plan submitted by a local architect named James Craig. The plan's chief features were two large squares, linked by a broad thoroughfare and skirted on the north and south by two parallel avenues, one opening out to the fields farther north, the other, Princes Street, offering a splendid view of the castle to the south. If the leaders of Edinburgh wanted order, symmetry, elegance, and space, they had it in Craig's plan. If they wished to escape tenement life among cobblers and tailors, local builders provided them with private row houses, which began going up in the New Town shortly after Craig's plan was approved.

Though it was not completed until the early nineteenth century, the New Town was from the start an upper-class compound, something Edinburgh had never before had, and the consequences of this were far-reaching. With a ravine separating them from the old city, New Town residents were sharply isolated from the old hurly-burly of Edinburgh's common life. Indeed, the city soon ceased to have a common life, and by 1800 there were New Town residents who no longer came to the High Street at all. The city was split in two, dividing the rich from the poor, the learned from the unlettered, the polite from the raucous. The North Bridge could not span such divisions, and Robert Burns could not straddle them, try as he might. As winter came to an end, the poet had the uneasy feeling that he had worn out his welcome in Edinburgh, with his fortune still unmade. In the spring, sadder and presumably wiser, he returned to the plow.

Edinburgh flourished without him and even without the great men of its first great years, all of whom were dead before the turn of the century. Lesser men, on the whole, took their place, although the lawyer-novelist Walter Scott was a vast improvement over lawyer-novelist Mackenzie. Yet in many ways the early years of the nineteenth century were Edinburgh's heyday. It was then that the city became a magnet for scores of gifted, restless young Englishmen, a magnet all the more notable con-

Lady Stairs Close in Old Town, where Burns lived in 178

IN A HOVSE
ON THE EAST SIDE OF THIS CLOSE.
ROBERT BVRNS
LIVED DVRING HIS FIRST VISIT
TO EDINBVRGH. 1786.
479
LADY· STAIR'S CLOSE

The End of an Era

BIBLIOTHEQUE NATIONALE — PHOTO BULLOZ

Sir Walter Scott

Old and new Edinburgh coalesced in the person of Walter Scott. He was born in a third-floor flat of a tenement in the Old Town in 1771; he died, in 1832, as the city's golden age was nearing its end. Scott partook freely in the life of his city: he drank with the best of the sots, joined his fellow advocates in pleading cases before the bar, marched with zeal as a volunteer cavalry officer, and was an early contributor to the Edinburgh Review. *Though a man of the Enlightenment, he was also the purveyor of an ancient, and violent, tradition, for he was convinced that Scottish nationalism could be reasserted through the poetry, songs, and legends of the gallant Highlanders. In his best novels, like* The Heart of Midlothian, *he combined his interests in nationalistic antiquarianism and enlightened progress, seeking to judge "the past by the present and the present by the past."*

The "heart of Midlothian," set into the pavement of High Street, commemorates the site of the Old Tolbooth prison.

sidering that the young men's fathers and grandfathers had probably looked upon all Scots with loathing and contempt. In 1811 Shelley and his first wife, Harriet, spent their honeymoon in Edinburgh, at 60 George Street in the New Town. Lord Palmerston, future prime minister of England, went to Edinburgh to attend Dugald Stewart's famous lectures on philosophy. Young Charles Darwin attended Edinburgh's medical school, by then the finest in the world, and acquired his taste for geology at the Royal Society of Edinburgh.

With the New Town fully occupied, newer new towns began rising, along with handsome classical public buildings. If the old grim High Street had ceased to be the common concourse, Princes Street partially replaced it. Even crusty old Thomas Carlyle fondly remembered the street's daily four o'clock promenades.

> All that was brightest in Edinburgh seemed to have stept out to enjoy, in the fresh pure air, the finest city-prospect in the world and the sight of one another, and was gaily streaming this way and that. The crowd was lively enough, brilliant, many-coloured, many-voiced, clever-looking (beautiful and graceful young womankind a conspicuous element); crowd altogether elegant, polite, and at its ease tho' on parade. . . . It was finely convenient to a stranger in Edinburgh, intent to employ his eyes in instructive recreation; and to see, or hope to see, so much of what was brightest and most distinguished in the place, on those easy terms.

In the short space of thirty or so years, Edinburgh had become a major intellectual force, a force exemplified in the extraordinary influence of the *Edinburgh Review*, a quarterly journal founded in 1802 by Sydney Smith and two Edinburgh youths, Francis Jeffrey and Henry Brougham. The articles in the *Review* were immensely long, invariably sober, and above all severely critical. The founders had chosen for the *Review*'s motto the Latin tag, "The judge is condemned when the guilty is acquitted," and by that motto the editors lived. Contributors to the *Review* never acquitted the guilty, though they did sometimes condemn the innocent. The young Romantic poets of England took such a severe beating in the *Review* that Byron wrote in protest his famous polemic on "English Bards and Scotch Reviewers," a testament to the enormous influence that the *Review*—and Edinburgh's savants—then wielded.

Yet the *Edinburgh Review*'s utter failure to appreciate the English Romantic poets was more than a mere aesthetic blind spot. It was a symptom of something far deeper and more serious: the decline of Edinburgh's classicism into something smug, rigid, and lifeless. Back in 1766 the city's love of classical ideals had had the force of a genuine rebellion, a rebellion against the gloomy tenets of Calvin and Knox, a rebellion against cruelty, bigotry, and fanaticism. By the third decade of the nineteenth century, Edinburgh's classicism had become pedantic, the pedantry displayed, for example, in the monument to Dugald Stewart modeled on an ancient Athenian monument to Lysicrates.

In the New Town, the ideals of elegance and refinement were dwindling into fussy gentility. The cozy old society of supper parties existed no longer; it had grown a trifle too "familiar" for latter-day Edinburgh tastes. At the very moment when the city's proud natives were beginning to call Edinburgh the "Athens of the North," it had ceased, in every important way, to deserve the title. With Walter Scott's death in 1832, the last great native son of Edinburgh passed away and the golden age was over. That, of course, was inevitable. Golden ages never last, but how many cities have a golden age at all?

Scott's Monument in the Princes Street Gardens

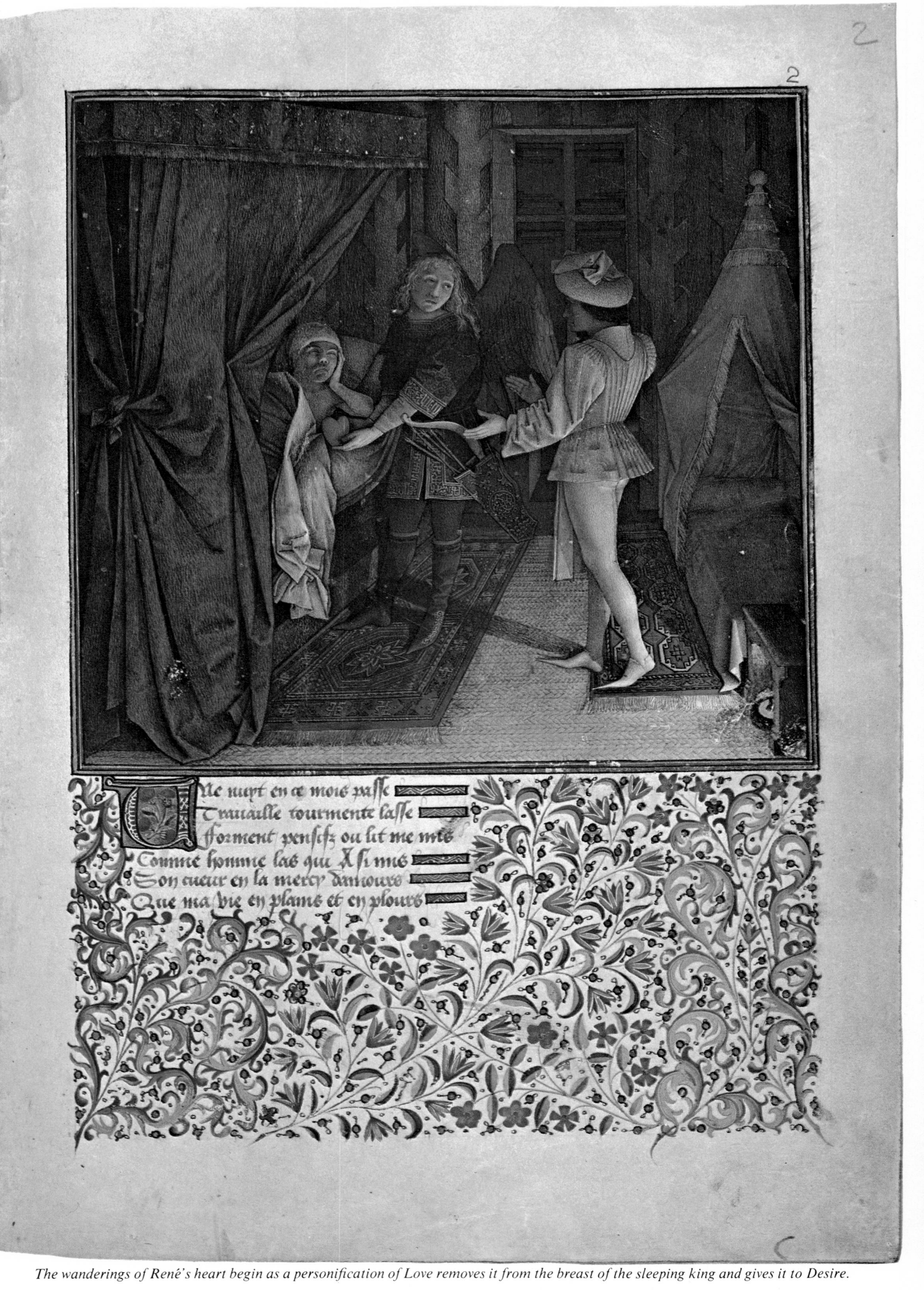

The wanderings of René's heart begin as a personification of Love removes it from the breast of the sleeping king and gives it to Desire.

King of Hearts

René of Anjou and Provence spent a lifetime winning and losing crowns and kingdoms. But he left a courtly legacy—his book of love

He certainly was one for titles: thus, when, just over half a millennium ago, he drew up his will, he styled himself "King of Jerusalem, Aragon, and Sicily, of Valencia, Majorca, Sardinia, and Corsica, Duke of Anjou and Bar, Count of Barcelona, Provence, Forcalquier, and Piedmont," though all he actually controlled by then was Anjou and Provence, the other territories having, for the most part, been wrested from him. His life was, as one writer puts it, "a cascade of crowns won and lost."

But he was more than just a singularly unlucky contender in the dynastic wars that convulsed fifteenth-century France. He was a notable patron of arts and letters and an accomplished painter and poet. In particular, he was the author of a remarkable allegorical romance, *Le livre du Cueur d'amours espris* (*The Book of the Heart Possessed by Love*), some illuminations from the earliest manuscript of which, prepared under his supervision, are reproduced here.*

Known to history as René of Anjou, he is remembered in France—and with special affection in Provence—as "Good King René," a wise and well-loved ruler. He is also sometimes called "the last of the troubadours," because

BIBLIOTHEQUE NATIONALE

King René sits beside his bed, recording the dream that began with the event opposite; thus did he compose his Book of the Heart.

his verse celebrations of love and those composed and sung at his lively court revived memories of the vanished Provençal civilization that flourished between the tenth and thirteenth centuries. The two epithets, besides helping to explain why René cuts so attractive a figure, also point to a curious split in his makeup. For René, an enlightened and even liberal governor, was at heart a thoroughgoing romantic reactionary. In an age when Renaissance ideas were transforming feudalism, he remained steadfastly faithful to medieval ways.

René was born in 1409 at Angers on the Loire, the third child of the duke of Anjou. At ten he was married to the nine-year-old Isabella of Lorraine, and at twenty he fought under Joan of Arc against the English occupiers of northern France. The following year, on the death of a great-uncle, he became duke of Bar in eastern France, and a year later, when Isabella's father died, he claimed the much larger neighboring duchy of Lorraine. A vassal of the powerful duke of Burgundy, however, disputed his claim; their forces clashed, and René, captured, was imprisoned in a tower in Dijon. Isabella obtained his release a year later by handing over their two sons as hostages.

In 1434 the death of René's elder brother made him duke of Anjou, count of Provence and Piedmont, and heir to the throne of Naples (or Sicily, the terms being interchangeable). He was also confirmed as duke of Lorraine by the Holy Roman emperor. Declining to accept the imperial appointment as valid, the duke of Burgundy recalled René to prison, where he spent his days exercising a talent for art by painting on glass. (He may have met the Flemish painter Jan van Eyck, then living at the Bur-

*A full-color facsimile of the illuminations has just been published by George Braziller, Inc.

By ORMONDE DE KAY, JR.

René of Anjou

René's heart was possessed by love more than once. He was only ten when he married Isabella of Lorraine, aged nine, and they lived happily ever after—or nearly so, for she died some thirty-four years later. René then wed Joan of Laval and soon afterward wrote his Book of the Heart. *Some see the somber ending of the story as reflecting the king's grief over Isabella; others think he may have been disappointed in his new bride.*

Joan of Laval

gundian court, and even taken lessons from him.) At last, in 1437, the duke of Burgundy freed René in exchange for money and lands.

Meanwhile the queen of Naples had died, and Isabella had been looking after René's interests there. On his way to rejoin her, an incident occurred that reveals much about his character. At Aix, in Provence, a certain Jew had blasphemed against the Holy Mother. Because of his youth the judges had simply fined him and let him go, whereupon an enraged mob had demolished a synagogue and was threatening to massacre every Jew in sight. Rushing to Aix, René dispatched the judges to Marseilles and took steps to put down the disorders. Once calm was restored he decreed a general amnesty; then, to forestall further anti-Semitic rioting, he declared himself protector of the Jews and issued regulations assuring Jews a tranquil existence in his domains.

Soon after reaching Naples and Isabella, René again became embroiled with a rival claimant, Alfonso of Aragon. For four years the struggle between them raged throughout southern Italy, but in 1442, ousted from Naples, he returned to France. Two years later he helped his brother-in-law, Charles VII, negotiate a peace with the English, sealing the compact by marrying his daughter Margaret to the unfortunate and intermittently insane Henry VI of England. He also settled another territorial dispute in the same way by marrying another daughter, Yolande, to the son of the nobleman who had fought him for possession of Lorraine.

Abandoning, for the moment, the profession of arms, René now turned to the cult of chivalry. In 1447 he founded a chivalric order, the Order of the Crescent, limited to fifty knights of impeccable pedigree, and stipulated that members must so comport themselves that "their praise and fame may ever be growing." He also compiled *The Book of Tourneys*, a compendium of the rules governing that favorite pastime of the medieval nobility. Magnificently illustrated in color—in part, perhaps, by René himself—it was soon accepted as the standard authority on the subject.

In 1453 Queen Isabella, René's wife for more than a third of a century, died. As if to blot out the heartbreak with action, he hurried south into Lombardy to help Milan and Florence against Venice, hoping to win their aid in an invasion of Naples, but the belligerents patched up their quarrel, and for a second time he left Italy in frustration.

René was now forty-five. Restless, lonely, at loose ends, he fell in love—like any number of aging leaders from Solomon to Strom Thurmond—with a woman less than half his age: Joan of Laval, the twenty-one-year-old daughter of a Breton nobleman, described by a contemporary chronicler as *"une très belle fille, vertueuse, sage, et bien conditionée."* In March, 1454, just twelve months after Isabella's death, he married Joan at Angers. The event signaled a fundamental change in his life style: henceforth he was to concern himself increasingly with art and architecture, literature and music, leaving dynastic ambitions to his son John. At his bidding, splendid country houses went up as residences for the royal pair. Wherever he held court—now at Angers or Saumur in Anjou, now at Aix or Tarascon in Provence—he surrounded himself with versifiers, painters, and sculptors, tapestry makers and master woodworkers, goldsmiths and silversmiths, musicians and entertainers. When not seeing to his subjects' welfare—by encouraging agriculture, notably, and striving to improve the universities within his domains—he busied himself laying out gardens and orchards and erecting arcades and pavilions, or delighted in fêtes, games, and country entertainments, in theatricals and evenings of music. He collected books in several languages, gave orders to a corps of copyists and illuminators, and himself drew,

OPPOSITE: *In his book, René's heart is personified by the Knight Heart, encased in armor and astride the steed Candor. Heart sets out with his page, Desire, in quest of the maid Sweet Grace. Here, having emerged from deep forest onto a grassy plain, they encounter Lady Hope in front of her splendid tent. She warns them of dangers ahead but assures them they can count on her aid.*

voulsist ou non si durement sestoit laditte dame de sa bride saisie
Donques quant il vit cela si descendit a pie et salua la da
me en luy demandant et priant quil luy ploust de luy dire qui
elle estoit ne pourquoy lavoit ainsi arreste Et dit en
telle maniere

Dame pour dieu que or vous plaise
Pour mon vouloir mettre a son aise
Amoy dire lac de vostre estre
Car sur toutes me samblez estre

Comment esperance tire le cuer hors de leaue et dit lacteur

Et quant le cueur se vit dehors sil fust ioyeux ce ne
fait pas ademander et regarda qui estoit celle dame
qui lauoit aide a yssir hors de leaue Si congneut q
cestoit dame esperance sa bonne maistresse qui ja autres
foiz luy auoit tant fait et ensaigne de biens Et adonc le
cueur osta son heaulme de la teste et abaissa la ventaille
et puis Ilz sentrebaiserent et sentrefirent tel feste et tel

21 v

painted, and even, it is said, composed songs and plays. He penned occasional verses, which he exchanged for those of his talented friend and fellow grandee Charles of Orléans. And he wrote long poems and romances.

Like René's crowns, several of the literary works long attributed to him were not really his. Even *Regnault et Jeanneton*, a pastoral that celebrates, under transparently disguised names, the love of René and Joan, is now thought to be the work of another hand. There are, however, two long works whose authorship by René is certain. The first, which he wrote a year or two after remarrying, is *Le mortifiement de vaine plaisance (The Humiliation of Empty Pleasure)*, a pious meditation recounting a sorrowing soul's conversion to God. And the second, written around 1457, is René's masterpiece, *Le livre du Cueur d'amours espris*.

That book—which, like its predecessor, is wholly medieval in conception, psychology, and style—closely resembles that classic among allegorical poems of love *The Romance of the Rose*, composed in the thirteenth century by William of Lorris and John of Meun. Like the *Romance, The Heart Possessed by Love* treats the great medieval theme of the Quest of the Holy Grail, except that here the Grail (or the Rose) is personified by a sweet young woman; as in the earlier poems, the action unfolds in the context of a dream, and the progress of the dreamer's love for his lady is described in terms of allegory.

One night, René recounts, he went to bed early, preoccupied with thoughts of love. In a dream René's heart, represented by the Knight Cueur (i.e., *coeur*, heart), sets out with his page, Desire, to liberate Sweet Grace from her three captors, enemies of love named Denial, Shame, and Fear. After parleying with Lady Hope in her country house and visiting the dwarf Jealousy in her hovel, traversing the Forest of the Long Wait, following the Stream of Tears from the Spring of Chance to the hut of the crone Melancholy—after these and sundry other peregrinations and adventures, Heart and Desire come to the sea, where they embark for the Island of Love in a boat piloted by two female sailors, Confidante and Accord.

On the island, the newcomers are shown by the prioress Compassion through the Hospital of Love, wherein languish celebrated lovers. The enumeration of the patients enables René to show off his erudition—and provides us with a fascinating glimpse into the medieval mentality, for many of these patients would hardly seem to us to fit the role: among the lovers are Paris, Theseus, Hercules, Caesar, Augustus, and Nero—along with Tristan and Lancelot; among the living lovers are Charles of Orléans, Charles VII, and, not least, René of Anjou. Behind the hospital is Love's cemetery, with the graves of such illustrious poets of love as Ovid, Petrarch, Boccaccio, and John of Meun.

Next day, Heart and Desire are welcomed to the Castle of Pleasure by the young God of Love and his mother, Venus. Obtaining the God of Love's permission to rescue Sweet Grace, Heart leads Desire and another companion, Generosity, to the Fortress of Resistance. They enter, and Generosity buys off Denial with purses filled with gold. Sweet Grace, meanwhile, has been notified of Heart's arrival by Compassion and Welcome, and she graciously accepts his homage. Only after Shame and Fear have been driven away, however, can Heart coax a kiss from his lady; then, accompanied by Desire, Modest Plea, and Compassion, he sets out joyfully with Sweet Grace for the Castle of Pleasure.

His joy is short-lived: on the way the party is ambushed by the enemies of love. Desire is slain, Heart badly wounded, Sweet Grace recaptured. Compassion takes Heart in charge: she comforts him, but warns him that he

OPPOSITE: *Having let Lady Melancholy lead him along the Stream of Tears to the narrow bridge called Dangerous Crossing, Heart has to fight the Black Knight Trouble, who guards the bridge against lovers. Trouble wins the match and dumps Heart into the stream. Melancholy vanishes, and Hope reappears. Here, true to her promise to help him, she pulls Heart back onto dry land.*

BIBLIOTHEQUE NATIONALE

Awarding the prize

Before The Book of the Heart, *René had composed—and possibly illustrated—his famous* Book of Tourneys. *Above, in a painting from that work, a lady presents a prize (under wraps) to the knight or squire who has fought most valiantly. René, who loved such ceremonies, also liked to move his court from one princely house to another. Among his favorite residences was the castle of Saumur, below in a miniature from the* Très Riches Heures *of his great-uncle, the Duc de Berry.*

MUSEE DE CONDE, CHANTILLY-GIRAUDON

The castle of Saumur

VICTORIA & ALBERT MUSEUM, LONDON

The siege of the Castle of Love

A lady immured in a castle, her lover besieging it—this was a classic scene in the annals of courtly literature and art. In the fourteenth-century ivory above, the ladies on the battlement resist the knightly attackers by pelting them with roses. Below, in a miniature from one of several copies of René's book of love, Heart and his friends are about to enter the Castle of Pleasure, where Love dwells with his mother, Venus.

BIBLIOTHEQUE NATIONALE

Heart and friends at the Castle of Pleasure

must renounce Sweet Grace, who is doomed to linger in the power of Denial forever. Heart lets Compassion take him to the Hospital of Love, where he expects to live out his days in prayer and silent remembrance.

Just why this bittersweet love story should end on a note of nonfulfillment is a mystery, though one suspects—particularly since René's previous work, *The Humiliation of Empty Pleasure*, had also counseled renunciation and resignation—that his new young bride did not, after all, prove as willing a partner as he would have wished. We do know, however, that after completing the book he saw to the preparation of the manuscript—and of the exquisite illustrations shown here.

These miniatures, which have been called "a crowning achievement not only of French book illumination, but of book illumination in general," contrast surprisingly with the work they accompany, for they reveal an intensely modern spirit that anticipates the romantic sensibility and the new conception of landscape painting yet to come. The first miniature, with its play of candlelight in darkness, anticipates the art of Georges de la Tour; certain of the landscapes look ahead to Poussin; and some images are even like prefigurations of impressionism.

Did René himself paint these illuminations, which so magically evoke the terrain, architecture, costumes, and everyday life of fifteenth-century Anjou and Provence? It was long assumed that he did, but a more likely *Cueur* master would seem to be one Bartholomew of Cler—or Deick, as he is called in certain Provençal documents—a long-time friend of René's and one of the best artists in his employ.

René's last years were saddened by fresh losses. In 1461 his ally Charles VII died, and in 1470 his son John, on campaign in Spain, succumbed to the plague. Meanwhile, across the Channel, fate had dealt his daughter Margaret some hard blows. Her husband, Henry VI, had been chased from his throne in the Wars of the Roses, and she had fled to France; in 1470 he regained his throne, but the following year, with the Yorkists victorious, Henry was imprisoned in the Tower. There he mysteriously died, and Margaret, captured in battle, saw her only son put to death.

In 1474 René, in his will, divided his lands between a grandson and a nephew. Louis XI, aiming as always to bring all of France under his crown, retaliated by seizing Anjou. The historian Comines relates that René then plotted to spite the king by leaving his entire heritage to the duke of Burgundy, whereupon Louis haled him before the Parlement of Paris on an accusation of high treason. At last René knuckled under and swore never to ally himself with the duke of Burgundy. Louis returned his native duchy, settled a pension of 60,000 francs on him, and wooed his "good uncle" with shows of affection until René agreed to let Anjou become part of France on his death. Then he went home to Aix, and there, in July of 1480, he died, aged seventy-one.

René was widely mourned, for as one chronicler testified, *"Oncques prince n'ayma tant ses subjectz et ne fût pareillement aymé et bien voulu qu'il estoit d'eulx"* (Never did prince so love his subjects and none was in like manner so loved and wished well by them as he). But if his memory stayed green, the things he most cared about did not. Within a generation three climactic developments—the final triumph of Renaissance ideas in France, the discovery of the New World, and the Reformation—swept away the last vestiges of that medieval world of chivalry and *courtoisie* so dear to his heart.

There remains a final footnote to René's story. After his death, in accordance with his last wishes, his heart was removed from his body and interred separately. One senses that the Knight Heart, in the Hospital of Love, would have appreciated his creator's gesture.

OPPOSITE: *As Hope had promised, the Knight Heart reaches the seacoast; here he steps into a boat, manned by Confidante and Accord, that will take him and his companions to the Island of Love. His new ally, Generosity, one foot set on a rock, waits for his page to remove a spur, while Desire stands by. But their journey, alas, is to end in sorrow.*

Icy parle lacteur et dit ainsi que

A ces parolles le cueur Incontinent mist piet aterre
tout courroce et vergongneux de ce que tant auoit
amo et marcha droit ala mer et entra en la nas
selle et ses deux autres compaignons firent Incontinent ainsi
et habandonnerent tous leurs cheuaulx aleurs varletz qui
les prirent et les emmenerent pour le guerredon de leurs ser

51v

Hunger and History

The first recorded famine occurred in Egypt in 3500 B.C. Since then, uncounted millions have died, and still die, of starvation. Herewith, a cluster of essays proving, in sum, that there is more to famine than a lack of food

In the search for food humanity has gone to astonishing lengths—migrating into unknown lands, killing and even taming dangerous animals, coaxing recalcitrant shoots to yield a little more grain from one year to the next, and settling down, however reluctantly, into the relentless toil of farming. Yet hunger is always at the door, even in an era like ours, which can measure both its nuclear and its agricultural yields by the megaton. Do people starve simply because there are too many of us? Or because famine is the ineluctable companion of civilization? Was Parson Malthus right in his grim insistence that population must necessarily outdistance food supply? Or, in fact, do the hungry die of politics? Four frequent contributors to HORIZON present some answers, in the light of history.

The First Food Crisis

By JOHN PFEIFFER

Man's first major food crisis occurred before written records, before the coming of crowds and mass production and cities. It began 10,000 to 15,000 years ago, when there were fewer people in the whole world than there are today in New York City. It produced man's first and in many ways most drastic revolution, the shift from hunting and gathering to agriculture, from a nomadic life to a settled farming existence.

That a food crisis lay at the root of this far-reaching transformation is a relatively recent discovery. In fact, it has not yet made the textbooks. It involves a complex chain of events: gradually increasing populations, the submergence of great stretches of land under water; and some still unexplained results of people settling down. The discovery is based on new archaeological finds and new interpretations of old finds, and on continuing studies of today's few and fast-vanishing hunter-gatherers—studies that have enormously increased our respect for them and for their, and our, remote ancestors.

The new outlook represents a rather sharp break with the past. The tendency not long ago was to regard all surviving hunter-gatherers with condescension at best, an attitude implicit in the widely accepted ideas about agricultural origins. According to the once-popular Eureka! theory, for example, it all began with a lucky accident. Wild seeds fell on disturbed soil near an occupied cave, took root, sprouted, and happened to catch the roving eye of a prehistoric genius who suddenly saw the possibilities of deliberate planting and cultivation.

The theory appealed to many investigators, among the most distinguished being Charles Darwin himself, and it still has its proponents. It is, however, highly problematic, and highly uncomplimentary. For one thing, it assumes that even after tens of thousands of generations, our ancestors were still too dimwitted to know what happens when a seed is planted and, until that flash of springtime insight, had never experimented with cultivation. (Actually, the Neanderthal people and their predecessors almost certainly knew a good deal about gardening 75,000 or more years ago.) Even more belittling is the assumption that, once enlightened, they would of course leap at the chance to become farmers, the inference being that nothing but sheer brute ignorance could possibly cause them to continue their miserable, lowly way of life.

Such notions, derived from imperial attitudes toward subjected peoples everywhere, began crumbling with the crumbling of empires—and with the first serious efforts to learn how hunter-gatherers actually live. A pioneer investigator, James Woodburn of the London School of Economics, set out as a graduate student nearly a generation ago to study the Hadza, an African tribe occupying an isolated valley in Tanganyika (now Tanzania) some two hundred and fifty miles south of the equator. He did not receive much encouragement. The report of a British colonial officer assured him that the typical Hadza was "apelike," "a wild man," "a creature of the bush . . . incapable of becoming anything else." His professors told him that the tribe no longer existed, a bit of misinformation confirmed by local authorities in Tanganyika. But he went into the back country anyway, found the Hadza, and lived with them for more than three years.

It turns out, not surprisingly, that they know what is growing on every square foot

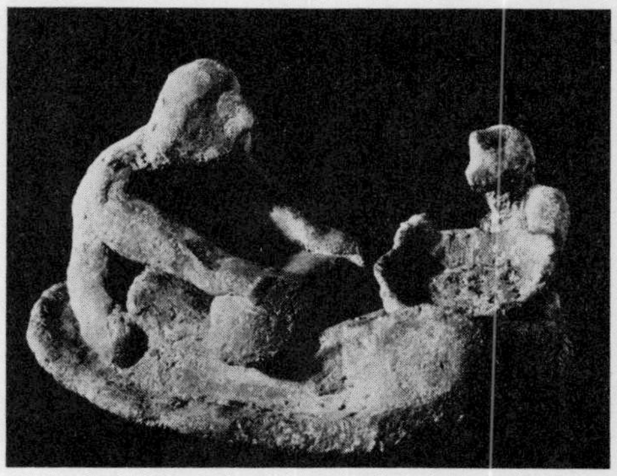

The solid gold stalk of wheat, opposite, was fashioned by a Greek artisan in about 300 B.C., perhaps for a tomb as a symbol of everlasting life, or as an offering to the goddess Demeter. In the homely clay figurine from ancient Cyprus, above, a woman grinds grain as her daughter, right, sifts away chaff.

HENRI LHOTE

In a prehistoric rock painting from the Sahara, above, two antelope, superimposed on the neck of a giraffe, are pursued by a hunter. The once verdant Sahara eventually dried up, and the wasteland still moves southward, bringing famine to the millions settled on its borders. Like their ancient forebears, the twentieth-century Bushmen below, in a part of southern Africa where food can still be found, feed themselves by a few hours of hunting and gathering each day.

THE AMERICAN MUSEUM OF NATURAL HISTORY

of their home territory and are quite realistic about what it offers. They eat roots, tubers (including a relative of the sweet potato), berries, honey, the fruit of the baobab tree, and an occasional antelope, giraffe, or zebra steak. They are by no means overjoyed with this selection, considering much of it unpalatable, and speak feelingly about being hungry for "real food," namely, more red meat. Furthermore, they are quite aware that farming tribes subsist on more appetizing foods. But the mere suggestion that they try farming themselves, even on a small scale, evokes incredulous, you-must-be-joking reactions. It makes no sense to go to the trouble of growing crops, which frequently fail, when roots and berries are available all the time in ample quantities.

The more Woodburn learned about the Hadza, the more he appreciated their point of view. They devote no more than two or three hours a day to the quest for food, and then spend the rest of their time resting, visiting, and playing games. Apparently it is a healthy as well as a leisurely life. When pediatricians from the Makerere College Medical School in Uganda came by to examine the Hadza children, they pronounced them "one of the best nourished groups in East Africa."

Investigators report a similar affluence among the Kalahari Bushmen of southern Africa, the Australian aborigines, and other twentieth-century foragers. The record is even more impressive when you realize that they are living on arid, third-rate land that nobody else wants. Things must have been considerably better in prehistoric times. So the hunting-gathering life turns out to be anything but nasty, brutish, and short. In certain respects it is the best way of life ever invented, and it served our ancestors well for more than five million years.

All the evidence adds up to one basic point. People changed not because they wanted to but because they had to, for the most vital of reasons: certain foods were becoming scarcer, and more severe scarcities were imminent. An archaeological sign of the changes was a kind of "freezing," a loss of mobility. Imagine a large wall map of the world with sets of animated lights designed to indicate how most people obtained their food 10,000 to 15,000 years ago. The lights are in rapid motion everywhere, representing hunter-gatherers on the go, moving from place to place as they deplete local resources or follow herds of big game or explore new terrain.

Now imagine the state of affairs five or six millenniums later. Over most of the map's surface the lights are moving very much as they moved in the previous display, yet there are some notable differences. The general pace of things has changed in parts of the Near East, Europe, India, Southeast Asia, and China. The lights do not move as fast or as far, and in a few places—the eastern shore of the Mediterranean, the highlands of western Iran, the limestone cliffs of southwestern France —the lights do not move at all.

People had to stop moving because at last the world was beginning to fill up. The problem of getting enough food had been postponed—literally—for ages. A less clever species would have been forced to face the music much sooner, but man kept delaying that day of reckoning by spreading into semidesert regions, humid tropical rain forests, subarctic plains, and the thin air of high mountain valleys.

Other powerful delaying forces had been at work, too. Natural causes such as disease and accidents killed about one out of every two infants before the end of the first year of life, and also killed a sizable proportion of older individuals. Yet even that heavy toll could never have held things within bounds. Unless man himself had deliberately taken extra control measures, the world would have been overcrowded long ago. He limited his numbers further by resorting to abortion, infanticide, and a variety of sexual taboos.

And still populations increased, although so slowly for such a long period that the rise was barely perceptible. According to one calculation, prehistoric man's annual rate of growth was only about .001 per thousand, which means that it would have required about a millennium for a population of a thousand persons to increase by just one additional member. (Our current annual growth rate is about twenty thousand times greater, and the same increase occurs now in less than three weeks.)

It was that extremely small growth rate, however, compounded over millions of years, that provided the driving force for the spread of our kind over the earth.

Bands of hunter-gatherers stayed small by splitting, as pioneers kept migrating to new frontiers. Assume that in the beginning, say about five million years ago, the world contained some twenty-five thousand members of the family of man (a sheer but not implausible guess allowing for the fact that our kind may still have been a minority breed confined to a few parts of Africa). At an annual growth rate of .001 per thousand, the figure would have increased to some ten million persons by 10,000 B.C. That comes to several hundred thousand bands at large in the wilds of Europe, Asia, Australia, and the Americas as well as Africa, just about the total arrived at in rough estimates based on the number of prehistoric sites.

By modern standards a world population of ten million, or about one person for every five and a half square miles of the earth's land surface, can hardly be regarded as densely packed. But the situation looks rather less spacious from a hunter-gatherer's point of view. Crowding is always a relative thing, especially when you consider the state of the art of obtaining food in those days. Yields of wild plants and animals were such that it required about one square mile to feed one person. People were beginning to feel the pinch.

To make matters worse, available land was decreasing as populations increased, a point emphasized by Lewis Binford of the University of New Mexico. In fact, the amount of land had been decreasing ever since the height of the last ice age some 20,000 years ago, when so much water was locked up in polar ice caps and glaciers that ocean levels were 250 to 500 feet lower than they are today. Hunter-gatherers wandered over the exposed continental shelf, a system of sloping plains that form a rim up to 800 miles wide around the ocean basins.

Then the glaciers started melting. Water poured back into the seas, ocean levels rose, and year after year successively higher high tides inched farther up the slopes of the continental shelf. Within a few millenniums an inexorable glacial flood had submerged millions of square miles of fine hunting-gathering territory, an area about the size of Africa, or nearly a fifth of the total land surface. As far as human living space was concerned, the world had become appreciably smaller.

The pressure was on. Rising seas and rising populations increasingly deprived people of the old option of moving on. When land or food had been in short supply, when there were too many mouths to feed, some of the people had always packed up and left friends and relatives behind. They walked toward passes seen dimly on the horizon, always finding new abundance in the next valley. Think of what a shock it must have been the first time they looked down, saw campfires burning below, and realized that the next valley was occupied.

The new order of things is documented at many sites. Jean Perrot of the French Archaeological Mission in Israel has reported some of the world's oldest permanent dwellings at Mallaha, a site located about twenty-five miles from the Mediterranean coast and not far from the Sea of Galilee. Here, among the ruins of a little village, you can see that people had settled down permanently. There are round houses built on stone foundations more than twenty feet in diameter, traces of flagstone paving, and plaster-lined storage pits.

Perrot, who has excavated about half an acre of the site, calls it "a paradise for prehistoric settlers." They went after local food in marshlands, lake country, and mountain valleys. They used fishhooks, harpoons, mortars and pestles, and flint bladelets, still smooth and lustrous with "sickle sheen," produced by abrasion against the silica-containing stalks of grasses. They arrived around 10,000 B.C. and established a community of some hundred and fifty persons; it endured for at least a thousand years and perhaps twice as long.

The most significant thing about Mallaha and sites like it is what they tell us about how people behave under subsistence stress. There is absolutely no evidence of domestication. Instead, people were exploiting their home territories more and more intensively, relying more and more on fish, small game, seeds, migratory birds, and other foods once used in comparatively small quantities. And they were fighting for their land as never before. The oldest unequivocal records of man using weapons to kill man—flint points found imbedded in skeletons—date to this period.

But, and this is the main point, they were still hunter-gatherers. With an age-old tradition behind them, they did not want to change, to sow and weed and harvest and build fences to keep animals in and people

The Carnivorous European

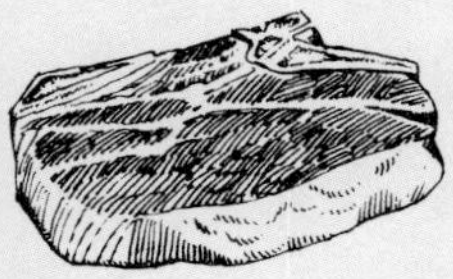

DRAWINGS BY CAL SACKS

Much has been made lately—and with good cause—of the inefficient way the wealthy nations get their protein. Americans, for example, get much of theirs from beef, which requires a wasteful twenty-one pounds of grain for each pound of meat. Substitute protein sources have been proposed—beans, cats, dogs, possums, and even grilled termites, which are said to contain more than 45 per cent protein.

Yet the habit of eating meat is an ancient one, and hardly peculiar to modern or even wealthy societies. In that remarkable work, *Capitalism and Material Life, 1400–1800,* Fernand Braudel remarks that "the broad outlines of man's dietary history are marked and controlled by two ancient revolutions. At the end of the Paleolithic Age the 'omnivores' moved on to hunting large animals. 'Great carnivorism' was born and . . . has never disappeared." The second revolution was the invention of agriculture, which, while reducing large numbers of people to a vegetarian diet, made it possible for others to raise livestock. Thus was humanity divided into two dietary categories—and Europeans have definitely preferred the carnivorous sector. Furthermore, writes Braudel, wherever Europeans have traveled, they have demanded their tastes be catered to. "Abroad, the lords and masters ate meat."

The Villainous Potato

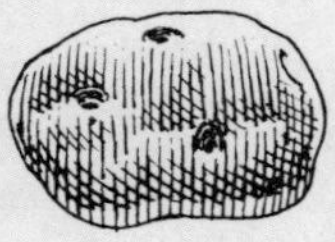

The history of the potato (*Solanum tuberosum*) is linked closely, perhaps even ominously, with our own. Introduced into Europe by sixteenth-century Spanish explorers who had come upon it in Peru, it was (along with maize) the first true miracle crop. If served occasionally with milk, it was a completely adequate diet, and an acre and a half of potatoes would feed a family of six year round. The poor at first resisted it as a dietary staple, but it gained a reputation as a curative and as an aphrodisiac. According to one seventeenth-century English commentator, potatoes "nourish the whole Body, restore in Consumptions, and provoke Lust." By the end of the eighteenth century, the root was a major crop throughout Europe, and —according to historian Fernand Braudel—it put an end to widespread famines.

That was not all. From 1750 to 1850 the population of Europe almost doubled, and William L. Langer of Harvard lays the blame squarely on *Solanum tuberosum*. Even in the eighteenth century, a similar effect had been noted. David Henry, an English agriculturalist, observed that in western Ireland the potato was "favourable to population. . . . It is no unusual thing to see six, seven, eight, ten and sometimes more children, the issue of one couple, starting almost naked out of a miserable cabin."

out. But, with the best of intentions, they were making things worse all the time. By doing what they had to do, by staying put and digging in, they were unwittingly creating conditions that would speed the end of hunting-gathering.

The very act of settling down doomed that way of life. It caused a further increase of population, not the extremely slow increase of the past, but a genuine baby boom. Even today, with the advantage of hindsight and population research, we do not know precisely why this happened. The identical effect is taking place now among hunter-gatherers who have changed their life style in recent times. For example, David Harris of University College, London, has analyzed birth statistics for a group of aborigines living in northern Australia. There, between 1910 and 1940, mothers averaged one baby every 4.5 years. But when the people settled down, the average birth interval fell to 3.3 years, and there has since been a population rise of more than 33 per cent.

Apparently there is something about the nomadic life that acts as a birth-control mechanism. Perhaps, as Lewis Binford suggests, the upswing in offspring may be simply a result of the fact that village husbands are apt to be at home and available more nights than full-time hunters. Another possible factor, yet to be investigated, has to do with nursing customs. Active milk production inhibits ovulation, and if it can be shown that recently settled mothers do not nurse their babies as long as nomadic mothers, that might be part of the answer.

In any case, the population brakes were off. It was a slow process in terms of human life span, so slow that in any given generation nothing much seemed to be happening. But compared to the more gradual course of events during millions of previous years, the results were explosive. On the basis of excavations and site surveys in a 115-square-mile valley of western Iran, Frank Hole of Rice University, Kent Flannery of the University of Michigan, and James Neely of the University of Texas have come up with some estimates of the pace of change.

The first settlers in the valley, perhaps twenty people, arrived some time after 8000 B.C. and lived predominantly by hunting and gathering. Within a few centuries, however, their numbers had doubled or tripled. Even the most intensive hunting-gathering could no longer provide enough food for that many, and people began applying knowledge their ancestors had passed on for generations. They began to depend less and less on wild species and more on domesticated wheat, barley, lentils, peas, sheep, and goats.

Population continued to rise. By 5500 B.C. some four hundred people were living in the area, too many to be supported by food grown on naturally well-watered lands. One or two farmers, and later many farmers, dug channels and brought water from rivers and streams to previously arid places. Irrigated plots now produced higher yields, and within a millennium an estimated twelve hundred people were living in villages of up to ten acres, about the limit for the agriculture of the times.

During the same period the same sort of process was under way at different rates in lands across the wide Iranian Plateau, from the Tigris River to the Indus River and beyond, in Southeast Asia and China and Mesoamerica and the Andean highlands. Our ancestors, confronted with the first threat of universal famine, were moving into an uncertain future—and we, confronted with our own mounting shortages, can guess how they must have done it.

The odds are overwhelming that they backed into the future, protesting every inch of the way and never realizing the full significance of what was going on. The agricultural revolution was not led by revolutionaries, but by rock-ribbed conservatives struggling to make the world safe for hunting-gathering. Change came imperceptibly around evening campfires and hearths. People made decisions under pressure, coping with urgent here-and-now problems that might have been anticipated but rarely were.

Undoubtedly they devised prehistoric "rationing" systems, restricting hunters to certain seasons and to a limited number of animals. Despite some poaching, things improved for a time and the rules were relaxed. Later, under new pressures, people did a bit of extra planting and, still later, a little bit of irrigating. It must have been an unspectacular and often frustrating record of little scarcities, little adjustments, of stopgap measures accepted with much grumbling about ineffective leaders and much harking back to the good old days. In short, it was business as usual, at least until the next crisis.

The miracle is that this bizarre and mad process, sometimes fondly referred to as cultural evolution, did the trick. The land was supporting fifty to a hundred times more people than it had in hunter-gatherer days. Universal famine never materialized. On the other hand, the threat never disappeared either. Merely delayed, it faces us today, aggravated—the supreme irony—by our concern for the general welfare and the survival of infants, and our striking success in doing something about it.

The author is grateful to Mark Cohen of the State University of New York, Plattsburgh, for lending his new and unpublished study of population pressures in prehistory.

Food as a Weapon

By CHARLES L. MEE, JR.

"Where Ignorance is Bliss" is the title of the above cartoon, which appeared in 1846. At left, the Tory prime minister, Sir Robert Peel, feigning concern about the potato problem, quizzes Lord John Russell, leader of the Whig opposition, about the Irish famine. The lion bears some resemblance to Queen Victoria, who did little to aid the starving Irish.

Today's food shortages "could give the United States a measure of power it has never had before—possibly an economic and political dominance greater than that of the immediate post-World War II years. . . . In bad years, when the United States could not meet the demand for food of most would-be importers, Washington would acquire virtual life-and-death power over the fate of the multitudes of the needy."

—Office of Political Research,
Central Intelligence Agency
August, 1974

Occasionally the world is struck by a disaster for which politicians cannot be blamed. Presidents and prime ministers are not, at least not always, responsible for climatic change, volcanic eruptions, plagues, or famines. Congress can neither declare an earthquake nor cut off funds in support of one.

Once a catastrophe occurs, however, politicians can potently determine its effects. Whether a disaster is to be unmitigated or mitigated, a disaster for all or only for some, whether a disaster is to harm or buttress established institutions, all these are political questions. They arise today at a time of apparent world food shortages, as they arose in the 1840's when great crop failures shook Europe, and, with the help of the British Parliament, caused famine and death by starvation in Ireland.

In August of 1845, the British prime minister, Sir Robert Peel, received news from the Isle of Wight that the potato crop showed some evidence of "blight." For most of Ireland, the potato was not merely the basis of a diet, it constituted the whole of the diet. The blight, caused by the fungus *Phytophthora infestans*, turned the potato fields black and transformed potatoes into a rotten mass "from which so putrid and offensive an effluvia issued that in consuming it [the Irish] were obliged to leave the doors and windows of their cabins open." When the diseased potatoes could be eaten at all, they caused dreadful illness, and even killed hogs and cattle. Beginning in the autumn of 1845, the blight spread quickly, and, during the following three years, completely. Tenant farmers, their crops ruined, were unable to pay their rents, were evicted by scores and hundreds, and took up residence with their families in holes dug in the earth and covered with turf. When these refugees were found in their holes, they were chased on to dig other holes.

Even in an ordinary year, nearly a third—more than two and a quarter million—of the Irish were unemployed, except for the brief period when potatoes were cultivated. The blight struck a people who were, in the best of circumstances, poor and hungry, living in the most densely populated country in the world, where couples had to have six children to guarantee the survival of two children past the age of five. The property of the fortunate Irish laborer, according to a government report, consisted of a pig and a manure pile.

The only hope for Ireland, as Sir Robert Peel instantly perceived when the blight appeared, was massive importation of grain. Unhappily, no grain of any kind—wheat, oats, barley—could be imported without the repeal of the Corn Laws. As Cecil Woodham-Smith records in *The Great Hunger*, "The purpose of the Corn Laws was to keep up the price of home-grown grain. Duties on imported grain guaranteed English farmers a minimum and profitable price, and the burden of a higher price for bread was borne by the labouring classes. . . ." Curiously enough, this economy, controlled though it was by such devices as the Corn Laws, was called a laissez-faire, free enterprise economy, and Parliament was determined to preserve it.

The Corn Laws were important not only in and of themselves but also as a symbol of protection of the propertied class and thus of the bases of the English economy and government, which were run by men of property. To undermine grain prices, therefore, was thought to undermine the very foundation of the country.

Nonetheless, common decency and political prudence required that at least some relief be given to the Irish, and Peel's strategy to bend the system was ingenious: he organized a public works program for Ireland, and the Irish were put to work building unnecessary roads, repairing harbors, and laboring on drainage projects. With the money thus earned, they could buy grain. Since there was no established trade in maize from America, the government, working through private traders, imported maize without disturbing existing grain markets. Yet, for all the brilliance of the plan, it could not suffice. Public works took too long to start up, and the wages were too low; for fear of disturbing private enterprise, too little maize was imported.

Paradoxically, throughout the famine, Ireland exported grain to England. Irish farmers ate potatoes; indeed, they had to eat potatoes. The grain they produced they sold to pay their rents; if they did not sell their grain, their landlords would evict them from their farms; if they were evicted, they lost their livelihoods, their houses, and their potato fields, which, while worthless in 1845, might feed them in 1846. (Landlords, of course, might voluntarily have postponed collection of rents, and a few landlords did just that. Most, however, were chary of upsetting traditional relationships with their tenants, and the government generally agreed with the landlords.) And so, while the Irish starved, grain was shipped to England. As Charles Edward Trevelyan, head of the English Treasury in the 1840's, declared, "Do not encourage the idea of prohibiting exports . . . perfect Free Trade is the right course."

Then, on February 16, 1846, the Horticultural Society of London was shown the first samples of the new, 1846 crop, "in which the disease had manifested itself in a manner not to be mistaken." The crop failure of 1846 was destined to be even more severe than that of 1845. Trevelyan's reaction was immediate. Government relief programs must be closed down, he said: "The only way to prevent the people from becoming habitually dependent on Government is to bring the operations to a close."

Most of the Irish easily avoided becoming dependent upon the government. They pawned their clothes and bedding to buy food. They ate boiled cabbage leaves, roots, weeds, and nettles. Children were put in workhouses where, in Skibbereen at least, more than half of them died. Thousands of beggars roamed the streets of Cork where, according to Woodham-Smith, they died "at the rate of one hundred a week." A magistrate in Cork wrote to the duke of Wellington:

> I entered some of the hovels. . . . In the first, six famished and ghastly skeletons, to all appearances dead, were huddled in a corner on some filthy straw. . . . I approached with horror, and found by a low moaning they were alive—they were in fever, four children, a woman and what had once been a man. . . . In a few minutes I was surrounded by at least 200 such phantoms, such frightful spectres as no words can describe. . . . Their demoniac yells are still ringing in my ears. . . . The police opened a house on the adjoining lands, . . . and two frozen corpses were found, lying upon the mud floor, half devoured by rats.

The starving Irish were too weak from hunger, or too accustomed to subjection, to rise in violent revolt; but in Roscommon, some three hundred starving men staged a protest march, and were scattered by two troops of mounted Dragoons.

In 1846, crops failed all over Europe. Wheat, oats, and barley were in exceedingly short supply, and rye and potatoes were a total loss. Even so, then as now, there was no absolute lack of foodstuffs. The Continental countries—with few of the laissez-faire inhibitions of the English—moved into the international market swiftly, bought maize, and drove up prices for all grain. In Europe in 1846, there was hunger, but no starvation to compare to that of the Irish.

The higher prices, said Trevelyan, were a "great blessing" that would help to limit consumption. But consumption hardly needed limiting. With little food available in any case, and little money to pay inflated prices, the Irish continued to starve, while grain ships were diverted from British ports to the Continent. In Kenmare, reports Woodham-Smith, Father John

As a young man, Sir Robert Peel (above at the age of fifty-three) served six years as secretary of Ireland and earned himself the enduring nickname of "Orange Peel" because of his Protestant enthusiasms—the same enthusiasms that would make the Irish mistrust him during the potato famine. The English cartoon below, published in 1845, entitled "The Poor Man's Friend," is erroneous only in that the poor of Ireland possessed no beds.

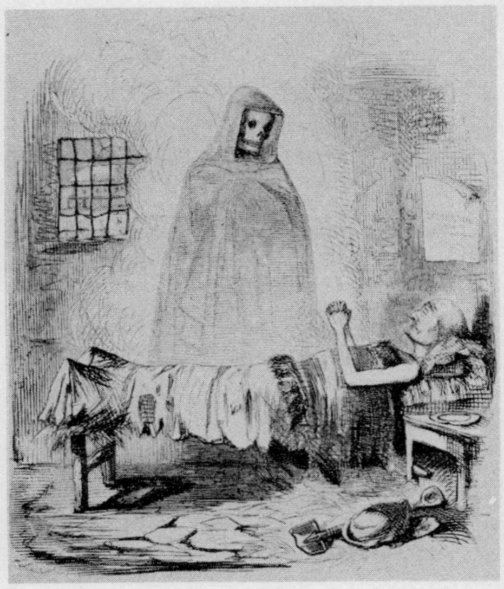

RADIO TIMES HULTON PICTURE LIBRARY

O'Sullivan "found 'a room full of dead people'; a man, still living, was lying in bed with a dead wife and two dead children, while a starving cat was eating another dead infant."

Some Irish rioted; some tried to form revolutionary groups; some tried to storm government grain depots, which were, on occasion, kept closed in order to avoid interfering with the free marketplace; some Irish killed their landlords; some engaged in pathetic terrorist tactics; most grew weaker and weaker from starvation. In 1847, typhus struck: faces swelled and turned dark, limbs twitched, high fever and delirium sent men and women jumping into rivers to cool their fevers; sometimes gangrene set in. Relapsing fever and fatal dysentery also plagued the wretched who huddled together in ditches and sod huts and workhouses.

Many of those who were strong enough to move—and had the money—emigrated. More than a million fled to North America; an even greater number went to Scotland, to Wales, and to such industrial English cities as Manchester. The "passenger trade" was a boon to private shipping companies. More than 100,000 Irish left their homeland for Canada in 1847, though only half of them survived the voyage and the ravages of the typhus they took with them. Not all of these starving beggars were welcome in their new havens, and the good people of Liverpool wished the Irish would go back home. But the Irish would not leave, and the threat of jail did not move them: "What is the good of committing them," asked one citizen of Liverpool, "when . . . gaol is a comparative Paradise to them?" Some of the Irish landlords complained that it was the best of the Irish tenant farmers who were emigrating, but Sir Charles Wood, chancellor of the Exchequer, greeted the news with equanimity as "a necessary part of the process."

Parliament had responded to the news of famine in 1845 with halfhearted attempts to ease the plight of the Irish; by 1846 the attempts were often less than halfhearted; by 1847, with famine still raging, the government had abandoned the notion of public works and turned to the organization of an inadequate number of inadequately supplied soup kitchens. Doctors warned that the watery stuff that was parsimoniously ladled out to the Irish was not sufficiently nourishing, and, for those who suffered from dysentery, was "actually injurious." But the government continued to dispense what one member of the Commissariat called its "drop in the ocean." Moreover, Parliament worried that inflation and other economic dislocations threatened a severe financial crisis, and so the Irish were told they would have to finance whatever emergency programs they had from their own taxes—if they could collect any.

In the spring of 1848, with famine still devastating Ireland, rebel movements sprang up all over Europe—in Sicily, Vienna, Milan, Venice, Paris. Governments collapsed, revolutionaries seized power, some of them drawing inspiration from the *Communist Manifesto* that Marx and Engels had published the year before. The British government feared that the revolutionary fervor might spread to Ireland. Whether coincidentally with this fear or because of it, the policy for Ireland changed from cool neglect to a program so thoroughly destructive that many have called it genocide. Estimates vary greatly, but the most conservative conclusion is that the Irish population was reduced in the 1840's—through death and emigration—by 30 per cent.

In politics, the first considerations of practitioners of the art are not always those of humanity. "To give food aid to countries just because people are starving," a member of America's National Security Council has said, "is a pretty weak reason." The business of politics is power, and politicians gain and hold power by using such instruments of pressure and force as economics, military might, and, if need be, starvation.

Ireland was, as much of the "Third World" is today, a nuisance—overpopulated, politically chaotic, unreliable, possibly threatening. In the 1840's, as today, there was enough food to avert starvation. Yet, distribution of the food seemed to pose a threat to the profits of some private traders and the economic dominance of the English; and, then, for political reasons, the English decided to reduce the nuisance of Ireland by reducing the Irish population. "I have always felt a certain horror of political economists," Benjamin Jowett said, "since I heard one of them say that he feared the famine . . .

The Wayward Press, 1846

The press, its own protestations notwithstanding, is not always an objective or dispassionate observer. In *The Great Hunger*, her classic study of the Irish potato famine, Cecil Woodham-Smith describes the editorial policy of English newspapers and magazines:

"English newspapers represented the Irish, not as helpless famine victims, but as cunning and bloodthirsty desperadoes. *Punch*, for instance, published cartoons week after week depicting the Irishman as a filthy, brutal creature, an assassin and a murderer, begging for money, under a pretence of buying food, to spend on weapons. 'With the money they get from our relief funds, they buy arms,' wrote [Charles] Greville.

"Ireland was a disturbing thought, and it was therefore a comfort to be able to believe that the Irish were not starving or, if some of them were, the depravity of the Irish was such that they deserved to starve; and to treat Ireland's desperate appeals, as famine approached, as merely another whine from a professional beggar. 'It is possible to have heard the tale of sorrow too often,' observed *The Times* leader-writer, on August 3, 1846."

would not kill more than a million people, and that would scarcely be enough to do much good."

In the end, not even children were given food. Men committed crimes just so they could get to jail and, they hoped, to jail food. Grocers dealt in dead bodies, to be consumed as food. Sir Charles Wood declared that "misery and distress should run their course." Others referred to the necessary "operation of natural causes." Mr. Twisleton, the Irish Poor Law commissioner, was blunter in his letter of resignation: the English, he said, had adopted a policy of "extermination."

After the winter of 1849, starvation and disease gradually abated. The blight became quiescent, new crops were edible, and harvests increased in successive years. The surviving Irish restored themselves to a level of poverty and hunger—with intermittent famines—and a new awareness that they were not dependent upon the English but subject to English domination.

Bitterness endures, and the Irish hatred of the English today, the current "troubles" in Ireland, cannot be explained without reference to the famine of 1845–1848—just as, perhaps one day, the famines of the 1970's will leave a similar residue of hatred in the Third World. "Half a billion people are starving," the London *Times* reported last year.

But forget about the human tragedy. Think of it the way the politicians do, and see it as a business opportunity. The producers best equipped to bridge the gap are the world's most efficient farmers, the Americans. But there are a hundred other countries determined to see that the crisis should not be a new opportunity for the U.S. once again to dominate the world economy.

Yet the Americans and the other producer nations are not the only political operators in the present crisis. Unlike the Irish in the 1840's, the leaders of the starving nations today resist trading political autonomy for food; they, too, many of them, would rather see their people starve than become subject to a foreign power. As in the 1840's, it is technically and physically possible to produce enough food to feed the world. But as in the 1840's, the prime considerations are political. As the American secretary of agriculture, Earl Butz, has said, "Food is a weapon."

The Persistence of Famine

By J. H. PLUMB

Fortuna, goddess of Fate

They stare at us from the newspapers; they haunt the weekly magazines—children with distended bellies and glazed, bulbous eyes; old people dying. Sometimes a skinny hand is held out without hope. Those in the photographs are dead, are dying, will be dead. Dead from one cause only: not enough to eat. Dead of starvation. Occasionally the *New York Times* prints a horrifying story of an old man or woman found dead of starvation in a Manhattan apartment, alone, unfed, a victim of the vast anonymity of urban life. Yet how rare it is for anyone in our cities to die that way—and how common elsewhere. The media bombard us with documentaries about the doom-laden areas south of the Sahara, where the desert steadily advances and the people die. Africa lives with famine: more people every year, more hunger every year. In India famine is endemic, kept not at bay, only barely in control, by massive injections of American grain. Two years ago China, perhaps Russia, were saved from Africa's fate only because they had the money to empty the granaries of the Middle West and Canada.

The harrowing pictures stir our conscience, for the children, the listless, downhearted adults, the pathetic elders, are always black or brown, never white. And we are told over and over again that famine will spread, that hunger will reach millions more every year. If we in the West gave up meat on just one day each week, we would release enough grain to stem the tide but, alas, not for long—half a year, a year maybe. Famine will persist. It will grow worse. The pictures of the doomed will continue to haunt us. But this is not new; it is only the return of a familiar visitor. Famine and mankind have lived together for millenniums.

It is hard for us to believe that famine used to sweep through the towns and villages of Western Europe almost every decade, garnering the young, the old, the weak. Europe, indeed, has known an abundance of food for a very short time, far shorter than America. Indeed, apart from Australia and New Zealand and a few tiny underpopulated parts of the world, the

United States is the only society in human history to lack the traumatic experience of famine. Even Europe did not defeat famine until the late nineteenth century, and then only in the West. France was one of the richest agricultural nations in Europe—vast cornlands in the Champagne, olive groves and vineyards in the south, lush beef pastures and great mountain plateaus for thousands of sheep: fertility everywhere, yet everywhere endemic starvation.

Pierre Goubert, who has carefully analyzed the condition of the peasantry in the Beauvaisis, has shown that the great majority of families scarcely possessed enough land to stave off starvation even in the best of times. Food was simple and bad—mainly gruel, a little cheese, and, more rarely, meat. So marginal was existence that four wet summers, from 1649 to 1652, brought devastating famine. Within ten years, in 1661, even greater disaster swept France: hundreds of thousands died of starvation in the worst famine of the century. Inevitably, famine bred pestilence as virulent diseases leapt from one enfeebled body to the next. Such great harvests of death were not, however, without their macabre recompense: bad times ended, and plenty, once returned, had fewer mouths to feed. But man, fertile as ever in the most gruesome times, replenished the population and thus created the prospect of renewed decimation.

So it was in most of Europe; only the Netherlands and England fared better. Farther east, conditions were worse. No decade passed without famine stalking the land. By 1750, only England had defeated famine: improved agriculture, an admirable transport system by the standards of the day, and a relatively small population made it one of the first countries anywhere to escape the scourge of famine. But not, of course, hunger: that still abounded, often desperate enough, as in Bristol in 1812, to drive men and women to riot.

But if England escaped famine, the British Isles did not, for Ireland, supporting too large a population on a single, too precarious crop—the potato—experienced not the worst but one of the most publicized famines of the nineteenth century—the Great Hunger of 1846. Over a million people, out of a population of some eight million, perished. Many were so desperate that they resorted to cannibalism—the usual by-product of desperate hunger. The misery was so profound, so traumatic, that it affected generations of Irishmen, breeding a deep hatred for the English, who, as absentee landlords, became the mythic fathers of the famine.

Yet the Irish famine was something of a turning point, for the British prime minister, Peel, spent large sums of government money to import maize from America to relieve the distress. Hitherto, famines had run their course, alleviated by small government benefactions and private charity. Direct government intervention to secure large grain supplies, combined with planned relief programs, was novel. Alas, the Irish did not know how to grind maize, and in any case were deeply suspicious of it, while the relief programs were hedged about with prohibitions. Nevertheless, in spite of its shortcomings, the operation became a model, later modified and improved, for the famine relief organizations that were a prominent feature in nineteenth- and twentieth-century Western societies.

By 1900, in Western Europe the battle was largely won: hunger there was in plenty, but no longer were tens of thousands of peasants dying. Eastern Europe fared less well, and of course even the precarious plenty of Western Europe could be, and was, destroyed by war. Germany and her satellites, as well as Russia, experienced famine after both world wars, and in 1919 the scourge of disease that goes with it swept through the West, killing more people by influenza than had been killed by bullets.

Along with organized relief went improvement in food production—a steady "green revolution" that began in Flanders in the early seventeenth century, burgeoned in England in the eighteenth, spread elsewhere thereafter, and still, thank God, possesses momentum. It was not merely an attempt to develop new land or improve crops and husbandry, it was a deliberate effort to increase yields, to experiment and disseminate the results. In England in the eighteenth century, technological development, of crops and machinery, was the self-conscious pursuit of an elite of landowners and farmers eager to improve yields and exploit new sources of food, such as the potato and the sugar beet. In the nineteenth century, America took the lead in agrarian advance, and the world's food supply, especially since the brilliant successes after

This detail from a fifteenth-century woodcut is Famine, the third horseman of the Apocalypse. According to the Book of Revelation, he rides a black horse, carries a balance, and is accompanied by War, Strife, and Pestilence.

World War II, has almost kept pace with the exploding population. In 1960 the people of the world were probably better fed than ever before.

Yet it was to prove but a moment of illusion, a mirage of plenty that the world is unlikely to know again. One sinister aspect of famine has always been that it only temporarily checks the pressure on a society's food supplies. The fertility of man, persisting amid the most terrible disasters and deprivations, soon obliterates the effects of famine relief and makes its recurrence ever more likely. Alas, a comparative abundance, combined with superior medical services, has had a like effect. Once more population growth, as in the past, has outdistanced not the good harvests but the bad, and bad there always are and will be. Drought in the Sahara, poor monsoons, crop failure in Russia and China—all have eaten up the world's reserves, and in Africa and India large-scale famine is once more reaping its harvest. And so humanity returns to the condition it has lived with for millenniums.

Food shortage not only kills people, it corrodes social institutions, breeding rebellion, violence, and locustlike migrations. Liberty and freedom are not born in hunger: it was famine that gave Lenin and the Bolsheviks their mass appeal. The constant peasant riots of seventeenth-century Europe served only to strengthen the power of the state, for they confirmed the need for professional standing armies, as much to keep a brutal peace at home as to make war abroad. Social turmoil usually leads to a strengthening of power at the center—sometimes in a monstrous form.

Observed in the light of the past, the prognostications are not good. Famine will stalk the world for the foreseeable future. And yet we should not be entirely without hope. The potentials for increased food production are not exhausted, and they are the preoccupation of highly intelligent men backed by government resources to an extent hitherto unknown. At least the problem is not left to Fortuna, the fairy godmother of famine. The horrors of Africa, the hideous pictures of starving Indians, these should not blind us to the fact that the world's largest population, the Chinese, have not suffered severe famine for a decade or more—a miracle by the standards of the past. And it is not impossible that these more desperate times may provoke a greater effort, a more relentless fight against one of the oldest enemies of man.

What we can be sure of is that the dream of plenty is over. It was scarcely ever more than an illusion. Man's drive to breed, so necessary for survival in a world of pestilence, war, and famine, becomes in a world of increasing supplies and improving health the procreator of the evils it formerly surmounted. In the seeds of birth lie the harvest of death.

A Specter at the Feast

By J. W. BURROW

Hope is the great consolation of existence, but like other more tangible consolations it is in variable supply. In Europe in the latter part of the eighteenth century there was a glut of hope. Certainly there was sufficient cause for Europeans to congratulate themselves on their achievements in recent centuries: the invention of printing, the discovery and colonization of the New World, the deciphering of nature's laws by Newtonian science, the application of power-driven machinery to manufacturing processes. No longer was it possible to believe that history always turned back on itself, that each cultural ascent was followed by a descent back to the starting point. Never before or since, perhaps, has an optimistic humanitarianism been so much the prevailing tone of a culture as in the late eighteenth century. Man's pride, and the source of all his hopes, was his reason. His task, privilege, and opportunity was to apply it to bettering his lot on earth. The end of superstition and ignorance was celebrated much as "the end of ideology" was proclaimed in the 1950's. Anonymous authors took as pseudonyms phrases like "A Friend of Humanity," "A Well-Wisher to Mankind." "Benevolence," "philanthropy," "feeling," and "sympathy" were cant phrases, like the jargon of a new religion.

The last decade of the century, however, was to deal some rude shocks to this humanitarianism and optimism—including a revolutionary Terror in France and the outbreak of the Napoleonic Wars. But another shock was provided, in Britain in particular, by a book, the work of a quiet English clergyman of placid temperament and admirable disposition, with an impediment in his speech. He was the Reverend Thomas Robert Malthus, and in 1798 he published, anonymously, an *Essay on the Principle of Population as it Affects the Future Improvement of Society*. Malthus's argument was that it affected it very seriously indeed. Hardship was and always would be the lot of the majority of mankind, because only by hardship, misery, and vice was population kept down to a level the supply of food could support. If Malthus was right, mankind, instead of surveying an enticing and illimitable prospect, was hemmed in by fate.

The cause lay not in some external obstacle but within man himself, in his own capacity and propensity to reproduce his kind faster than his environment could be made to provide nourishment. The source of this self-destructive power was located, by what seemed to Malthus's many critics an intolerable paradox, in the very source of life itself. The emotions apparently condemned by his theory were not avarice, cruelty, the lust for conquest, but the desire for home, wife, and family; the chain that bound mankind to its harsh fate was the wedding ring; the greatest threat to human progress was not armies or pestilences but a young man and young woman joining hands before the altar.

Out of these terrible paradoxes—in fact, a not altogether just version of what Malthus had actually written—was born the image of "Parson Malthus," a black-clad, thin-lipped specter at the feast of love and reason. Malthus seemed to personify the callous pessimism of the new "dismal science" of political economy, rebuking the poor as the authors of their own misery, condemning charity for aggravating, by sponsoring reckless breeding, the distress it tried to alleviate, scorning love, hating marriage—perhaps even a hypocrite who had himself fathered many children (Malthus "does the thing 'gainst which he writes," Byron mocked in *Don Juan*). As a picture of Malthus the man it was a grotesque caricature, but Malthus knew quite well what he was doing. The conflict between the outlooks of two generations, between the sentimental optimism of the late eighteenth century and the bleak realism of the early nineteenth, had occurred, though amiably enough, in his own family. Malthus wrote in his preface that his essay "owes its origin to a conversation with a friend." The friend was, in fact, his father.

Daniel Malthus—whose son Robert (his first name, Thomas, was never used) was born in 1766, one of eight children—was in many ways a typical product of eighteenth-century England: a cultivated, fox-hunting squire and an amateur botanist, rather ineffectual, a little pettish and disappointed, but an affectionate father and an enthusiastic believer in the perfectibility of man. He was a great admirer of Rousseau, whom he met during the latter's visit to England and for whom he tried to find a house near his own in Surrey. His enlightened enthusiasms were reflected in his choice of private tutors for Robert. One of them, Gilbert Wakefield, was a radical clergyman who was later imprisoned for expressing the hope that the French revolutionaries would come over and conquer England. Wakefield had been a Fellow of Jesus College, Cambridge, and it was there that Robert went in 1784 to read mathematics. After a successful undergraduate career he took clerical orders. He became a Fellow of the College in 1793, just in time to join the governing body that, in December of that year, passed judgment on an errant and debt-ridden undergraduate named Samuel Taylor Coleridge, who had run away from Cambridge to join the 15th Dragoons under the name of Silas Tomkins Comberbacke. Coleridge was to be one of Malthus's most hostile critics.

In his intellectual wrangles with his father, Malthus refused to share the dream of human perfectibility. It was the cool Cambridge mathematician against the sentimental optimist, political economy against Rousseau, and Malthus, obviously feeling that he had had the best of the argument, determined to present it to a wider public. The two radical utopians against whom Malthus particularly directed the arguments of the *Essay on Population* were the Marquis de Condorcet and William Godwin. There are few more striking testimonies to unshakable belief in human progress than Condorcet's *Sketch for a Historical Table of the Progress of the Human Mind*,* for it was written while he was in hiding from the French revolutionary government and completed shortly before his arrest and suicide. In the final

*See "How We Came to Believe in Progress," HORIZON, Summer, 1973.

NATIONAL PORTRAIT GALLERY, LONDON

Thomas Robert Malthus

In the satirical cartoon below, Mrs. Malthus interrupts the literary labors of her husband to offer him coffee. He protests: "Let me finish, Babet, I'm proving that those who are poor have no right to be hungry." To which Babet replies: "You will prove this between your first and second breakfasts."

THE BETTMANN ARCHIVE, INC.

part of his essay Condorcet looked to the future and saw there human happiness brought to a zenith by the triumph of reason and science.

Condorcet's English counterpart was Godwin, the husband of Mary Wollstonecraft, the father-in-law of Shelley, and, one might add, through the medium of his daughter's imagination the grandfather of Frankenstein. Godwin had been reared in the tradition of English Nonconformity, and some of the stark simplicities of that tradition clung to what he took to be the dictates of reason. Reason and natural justice were to be absolute sovereigns of human life, and what was left of the institutions of society—law, property, marriage—was very little indeed by the time Godwin had finished with them in *Political Justice* (1793). Godwin was not content with advocating; he was prepared to predict. In a state of equality the amount of labor required to support the frugal wants of rational men "is so light as rather to assume the guise of agreeable relaxation and gentle exercise, then of labour."

Condorcet and Godwin were Malthus's chosen antagonists; it was in fact an essay in Godwin's later work *The Enquirer* that had provoked the crucial argument between father and son. The beautiful mirages of equality, prosperity, and ease for all were to be swept away with two hammer blows: "population, when unchecked, increases in a geometrical ratio. Subsistence increases only in an arithmetical ratio." Malthus admitted that the formula was not absolutely exact. No tendency of the production of food to increase at the rate Malthus suggested could be demonstrated; but he assumed that he was stating the case for the potential increase in food production in the most favorable way possible by accepting the possibility that the produce of a unit of land might be doubled in a quarter of a century, and then increased by as much again in the following twenty-five years. His point was that even on this implausibly favorable assumption the capacity of human populations to expand was far greater, because each doubling of the population also doubled its potential for further expansion. The crucial phrase, as Malthus himself well realized, was "*when unchecked.*" Populations certainly do not normally increase in a geometrical ratio, and no one, including Malthus, supposed that they did. Why, then, did he think that the principle of population was such a knockdown blow to utopian beliefs, and why was his *Essay* generally taken to have been just that? Before looking at the answer to those questions we first have to put Malthus's *Essay* in perspective.

One of the things that makes Malthus's work a watershed is that throughout most of the eighteenth century, and earlier, the prevailing though not absolutely universal attitude toward expanding population was one of benign approval. Populousness was a sign of prosperity and civilization, of flourishing towns and manufactures. It was a source of military strength and useful labor power. Sparse population meant rudeness and barbarism, harsh lives and uncouth manners, plague, war, devastation. Religion and statecraft alike smiled on procreation: to bring children into the world, to replenish the earth and the muster rolls, was a religious and patriotic duty. In the later eighteenth century, however, a note of disquiet sounded, most notably in the work of Robert Wallace, another clergyman who foresaw the possibility that prosperity and good government might allow human numbers to "increase so prodigiously that the earth would at last be overstocked, and become unable to support its numerous inhabitants."

The point was sufficiently serious for Condorcet and Godwin to take account of it as a possible objection to their utopian predictions, but the bland confidence with which they dealt with it shows more clearly than anything else how great the impact of Malthus's essay was to be. Condorcet relegated the problem to a remote future and relied on human ingenuity to solve it if it ever arose. Godwin referred, as though to a mysterious but benign dispensation of providence, and with no inkling of what a terrible weapon he was presenting to his future adversary, to "a principle in human society by which population is perpetually kept down to the level of the means of subsistence." He had other suggestions too. A feature of progress would be a diminution of sexual desire: "One tendency of a cultivated and virtuous mind is to diminish our eagerness for the gratification of the senses." And finally, in an ideal society life might be prolonged indefinitely; the last

If Zero Population Growth is imminent for America, the large family will vanish like the dinosaur. Above, in 1940 at the New York World's Fair, wan parents preside over a banquet for their fifteen sons. And below, in 1974, Hugh Carey, then governor-elect of New York, carves a seemingly inadequate Thanksgiving turkey for his twelve surviving offspring and a son-in-law. In the quarter-century separating these two meals, producing this many children has come to be viewed as downright immoral.

WIDE WORLD

enemy would be put to flight, death would be abolished, and men "will probably cease to propagate."

One begins to see why Malthus thought he had a case, and why a mathematically minded clergyman in late eighteenth-century England, baptizing and burying the all too numerous children of the agricultural poor, as Malthus had done since 1792 as curate of Oakwood, in Surrey, might feel a certain impatience with his father's utopian sympathies. Malthus's rigorously logical essay is based on certain platitudes he thought Condorcet and Godwin had ignored. Certainly his initial assumptions are unlikely to be challenged:

"First, that food is necessary to the existence of man.

"Secondly, that the passion between the sexes is necessary, and will remain nearly in its present state."

The second is of course a hit at Godwin. Then Malthus springs his trap: "Assuming then, my postulate as granted, I say, that the power of population is indefinitely greater than the power in the earth to produce subsistence for man." The jaws of the principle of population close on the utopian hope: the tendency of population to increase is geometrical; subsistence can be increased at best only arithmetically. So much for Godwin's fantasies. The older eighteenth-century fears of overpopulation, including Condorcet's, are then revealed as altogether too weakly stated. Population that outruns subsistence is not a distant nightmare but a constant reality:

> By that law of our nature which makes food necessary to the life of man, the effects of these two unequal powers must be kept equal.
>
> This implies a strong and *constantly operating* check on population from the difficulty of subsistence. The difficulty must fall some where; and must *necessarily* be felt by a large portion of mankind.

The italics are mine, but the emphasis is the one Malthus intended.

At first sight Malthus seems to have made a set of platitudes yield a factual untruth. Population *had* increased, yet the incidence of actual famine in Europe had considerably diminished. Did this not run counter to Malthus's theory? The answer lay in the qualification to population increase: "when unchecked." Malthus realized that population and food supply had been, and could be, simultaneously increased, but he argued that their characteristic rhythm was an oscillation: any increase in food production and consequent decrease in the price of food would evoke a corresponding increase in population, until the closing gap between food supply and demand, expressed in a rise of food prices, checked the increase at its new, higher level. Political economy later made this oscillation even bleaker by applying to it the law of diminishing returns. Land being a fixed commodity, each extension of cultivation, being on worse land, would yield less food per unit of labor than land already under cultivation.

Malthus was not arguing that famine itself was the chief check. It was simply the final point, not often reached, in fact, on a descending scale of miseries: infant mortality, sickliness, epidemics, wars, and various disincentives to marriage and child rearing. The principle by which population was limited, "which Mr Godwin mentions as some mysterious and occult cause, and which he does not attempt to investigate, will be found to be the grinding law of necessity; misery, and the fear of misery." The checks, in other words, are either positive or preventative. Among positive checks Malthus includes wars and epidemics. The preventative checks he considered chiefly under the heading of vice: "Promiscuous intercourse, unnatural passions, violations of the marriage bed and improper arts to conceal the consequences of irregular connections."

For Malthus there were two major implications of his theory. The first was simply that until the human constitution changed in ways it gave no sign of doing, utopian hopes like those of Godwin and Condorcet—and, more to the point, attacks on the existing social order—were wildly impractical. If all men were guaranteed a modest subsistence as a right, this would simply encourage an increase in population, until, as a result of population pressure on scarce resources, inequalities and something like private property would inevitably re-establish themselves.

The second implication was that all measures for the relief of the poor were bound to fail: the Poor Laws, by making it possible for the poor man to rear a family he could not maintain by his own labor, actually created the poverty they were designed to relieve. It was this aspect of

Lifeboat Ethics

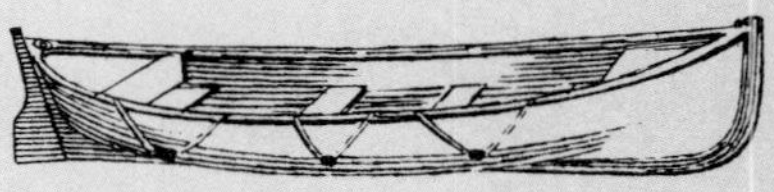

Over the centuries people have invented countless metaphors for the earth they live upon, calling it everything from a bountiful mother to a spaceship. Not until recently, however, has anyone thought to describe it as an overcrowded lifeboat.

But does the image not make a certain grisly sense? If there is too little food for the world's peoples, must not some suffer? And is it not the sad but inescapable responsibility of the rich nations to decide who? This is the argument put forth by Dr. Garrett Hardin of the University of California in Santa Barbara. Today, he says, there can be no such thing as justice for all: "The boat swamps, everyone drowns." Therefore, he argues, "for the foreseeable future our survival demands that we govern our activities by the ethics of a lifeboat, harsh though they may be."

Before congratulating Dr. Hardin for his tough-mindedness, we might examine the metaphor. Tarzie Vittachi, head of the United Nations World Population Year, maintains that the lifeboat analogy is false. "Far from being a lifeboat . . . the earth resembles a badly managed ocean liner." As long as there is still steak and whiskey in first class it may be too soon to order steerage to abandon ship.

Malthusian Paradox

It is a fair guess that population control, or attempts at it, are as old as civilized life. Infanticide and abortion were certainly among the earliest measures, though they cannot have been anything but repugnant, particularly to the women involved. The earliest known record of rational attempts at contraception is an Egyptian papyrus of four thousand years ago, which advocates the use of a mechanical barrier made of crocodile droppings. Variations of that technique have been used from that day to this, and the search for spermicidal chemicals began early, too. The ancient Greeks recommended frankincense mixed with olive oil, as well as peppermint juice and honey. In a sense, these measures are as "scientific" as any modern ones, unlike the amulets and nostrums and incantations that have had their vogue in every culture of the world. Quite recently, of course, medical research has come up with highly effective "barriers" like the IUD, as well as chemical spermicides and another type of preventative that the ancient world looked for in vain—the oral contraceptive. But these tools, including the various forms of surgical sterilization, will not, say demographers, suffice to prevent the world population from redoubling by the year 2000.

Malthus's theory that attracted the most hostility. To many there was something intolerably callous about the way Malthus seemed to deny the right of some people to be alive at all, and something distastefully smug about blaming the poor for their poverty. "What we ought to teach the poor," Malthus wrote, "is that they are themselves the cause of their own poverty: that the means of redress are in their own hands, and in the hands of no other person whatever." Malthus had made himself the spokesman not only of the social establishment but of the sullen men of property who resentfully supported poor relief.

Seldom has a single short book produced such an immediate effect as Malthus's *Essay*. Godwin was generally held to have been completely routed; his philosophical reputation collapsed. As for the Poor Laws, while Malthus's final triumph was delayed until the Poor Law Amendment Act of 1834, the year of his death, he nevertheless scored an immediate and flattering victory. Shortly before the publication of Malthus's essay, the prime minister, William Pitt, had proposed a form of family allowances, referring to "those who, after having enriched their country with a number of children, have a claim upon its assistance for their support." It was the last gasp of the old paternalism; he withdrew the proposal in deference to the views of Malthus and Bentham.

But it was not only Malthus's denial of the right to poor relief that incensed his critics. It was also the tone. He seemed to gloat over the miseries by which population was held in check, to rejoice in his destruction of the larger hopes of mankind. In the second edition of the *Essay* in 1803, a much more substantial work than the first, he added moral restraint to vice and misery on his list of checks. "By moral restraint I would be understood to mean a restraint from marriage, from prudential motives, with a conduct strictly moral during the period of this restraint" (he never mentioned restraint *within* marriage). If moral restraint could be fostered and late marriages encouraged, the prospects for mankind might, he allowed, be less bleak than he had at first indicated. Nevertheless, the picture he presented was still very far from the rosy prospects of equality and modest prosperity for all offered by the eighteenth-century optimists.

Much in Malthusian doctrine makes its author seem one of the more obvious harbingers of the Victorian era. The world he offers is one of close-fisted, tight-lipped thrift, rigid restraint and calculation, rugged independence and self-help. And Malthus did not mince his words, speaking with apparent complacency of "unhappy persons who in the great lottery of life have drawn a blank," and writing with what looked like cool effrontery that "a man who is born into a world already possessed, if he cannot get subsistence from his parents, on whom he has a just demand, and if society do not want his labour, has no claim of *right* to the smallest portion of food, and, in fact, has no business to be where he is. At nature's mighty feast there is no vacant cover for him."

Such language, not surprisingly, drew howls of execration and, in the ensuing years, attempted refutations by Robert Southey, William Hazlitt, Godwin himself, and a number of others. The kindliest caricature of Malthus was his portrayal, in Thomas Love Peacock's novel *Melincourt*, as Mr. Fax, who declares that "Bachelors and spinsters I decidedly venerate," and interrupts a rustic wedding to harangue the bridegroom on the evils of overpopulation (Malthus had suggested that a homily on the subject should be delivered by the clergyman as part of the marriage service). Others found Malthus hateful rather than whimsical. He was attacked by romantic Tories like Southey and Coleridge, who believed in a paternalist, hierarchical society like that of the Middle Ages, and by extreme radicals like Shelley, who continued to hold the Godwinian belief that poverty sprang from the maldistribution of wealth rather than from scarcity as such. It was William Cobbett, the radical pamphleteer, who castigated him as "Parson Malthus," saying he hated him more than any man alive. But even opponents paid a backhanded tribute to his influence: "For twenty years," Godwin wrote in 1820, "the heart of man in this island has been hardening through the theories of Mr Malthus"; and Dickens, in *Hard Times*, made Mr. Gradgrind call one of his sons Malthus.

Malthus himself seems to have been remarkably unperturbed by this chorus of execration. His conscience was clear: he did not, he indignantly said, advocate misery and vice; he merely described their effects. His attitudes on political questions were generally liberal rather than reactionary. He married his cousin Harriet Eckerstall, but the rumor that he had bred many times was baseless; he had three children and no grandchildren. In 1805 he became professor of modern history and political economy at the college at Haileybury, recently established to train young entrants to the service of the East India Company. He published books and articles on political economy, and died peacefully at Bath in 1834. All the witnesses to Malthus's private life agreed that he was singularly sweet-tempered, kindly, and equable, a man who quietly enjoyed life and in whose company others did the same; his students referred to him as "Pop." It is an oddly disarming reality to find behind the terrible "Parson Malthus." Malthus himself always insisted that the motive of his work was benevolence; there is no doubt that he hated poverty and never underestimated its sufferings. "The sons and daughters of peasants will not be found such rosy cherubs as they are described to be in romances," he wrote, and when he notes that plowboys, despite their occupation, seldom have calves on their legs, we seem to hear less the political economist than the observant curate.

The year of his death, 1834, was in some ways a turning point for Malthus's theory. The new Poor Law, abolishing outdoor relief and segregating the sexes in grim workhouses, was enacted that year; henceforth, as hatred for the "Poor Law Bastilles" mounted—Dickens said they offered the pauper the choice between starving slowly inside or quickly outside—the Malthusians were on the defensive. In the mid-nineteenth century a number of developments mitigated the Malthusian gloom. Britain proved able to support a greatly increased population by exporting manufactured goods and importing food. Emigration rose, and census returns showed a declining rate of population increase; perhaps, after all, prosperity might be correlated not with an increasing but with a diminishing rate of population growth. In the later nineteenth and early twentieth century there was even a revival of fears of population decline. In the stridently militaristic world before the First World War, population figures were seen as an index of national virility or debility: ironically, this was an attitude fostered by a distorted reading of Darwin, who had himself grasped the key to his theory of natural selection by reading Malthus's *Essay on Population.*

Finally, of course, what to the modern eye is the astounding omission from the Malthusian doctrine began to be openly advocated and freely practiced: contraception. There is evidence that Malthus knew of contraceptive methods and disapproved of them as unnatural. Condorcet had hinted at them in a passage Malthus primly (but almost certainly untruthfully) professed not to understand. There can be no doubt that he would have hated the use of his name in "Malthusian" or "neo-Malthusianism" as a euphemism for contraception and its advocates. But some of the younger political economists, notably John Stuart Mill, and radical journalists like Francis Place and Richard Carlile, were uninhibited by Malthus's scruples and deliberately set out to spread information about birth control, even though publications on the subject long continued to risk prosecution for obscenity. In the long run birth control transformed the situation in the Western world to a point where Malthus's doctrine seemed to have become blessedly irrelevant.

Nevertheless, Malthus's ghost will not rest, and to offer an appraisal of his ideas now turns out to be much the same as predicting the prospects for mankind as a whole. In the short term, in the West, Malthus was largely wrong and Godwin and Condorcet seemed oddly vindicated. The world's resources did seem inexhaustible; improvements in machinery, transport, and, finally, contraception did lift the majority of the populations of the industrial nations well above subsistence level. Affluence and a manageable population increase seemed not merely compatible but closely connected. Now, however, this way of looking at things has begun to seem uncomfortably parochial, and the terms of Malthus's inescapable ratios—agriculture, food, population—have re-emerged with a terrifying starkness. The shadow of Parson Malthus has lengthened ominously once again, and this time it lies across the globe.

Historian J. W. Burrow has written articles for HORIZON *on Marx, Darwin, and Bentham.*

The Pill vs. the Stork

Malthus saw "misery and the fear of misery" as checks on population growth, but was unwilling to admit that birth control measures might also play their part: the parson labeled them vices or "improper arts to conceal the consequences of irregular connections." Nor did he foresee that birth control would one day become respectable—even, as in these cartoons, a matter for casual public comment.

"When will it ever end, Miss Hartley? When will it ever end?"

Chaco Canyon's Mysterious Highways

There are nearly two hundred miles of them, built centuries ago by a people who had neither wheels nor beasts of burden. Like most superhighways, they seem to have created more problems than they solved

One day in the mid-1920's an archaeologist named Neil M. Judd was digging among the vast ruins at the bottom of a dusty red sandstone canyon in the northwestern corner of New Mexico. The site, called Chaco Canyon, was remote and not particularly hospitable. It lay one hundred miles from Albuquerque, in a region that was relentlessly dry (except for an occasional torrential thunderstorm) and all but treeless. Yet a thousand years earlier the ten-square-mile canyon, along with several thousand square miles of the surrounding San Juan Basin, had been the home of a people known to the present-day Navaho inhabitants as the Anasazi, the "Ancient Ones." There they had constructed vast pueblos with as many as eight hundred rooms, and lived lives that in many respects were as complex and interdependent as our own.

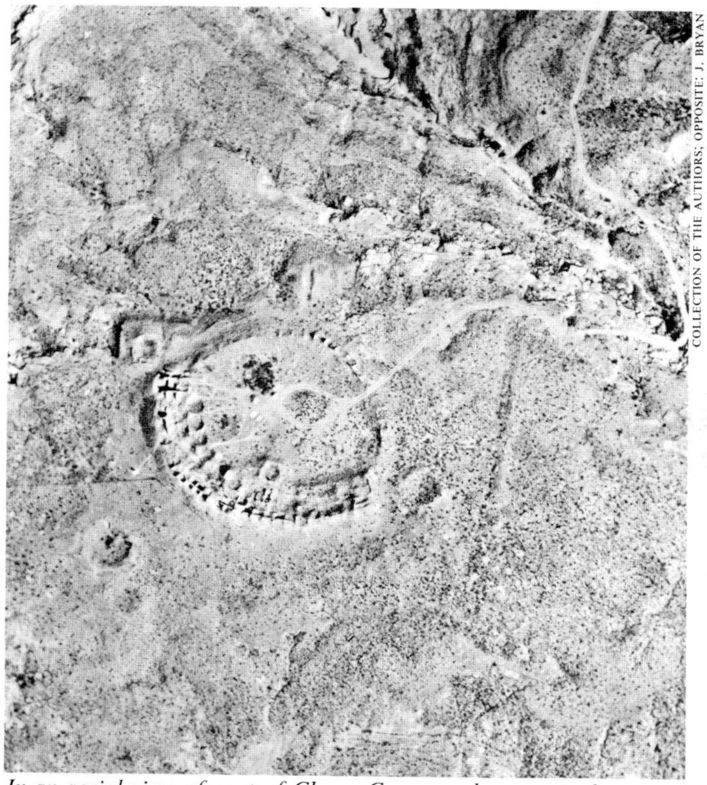

In an aerial view of part of Chaco Canyon, above, a modern road runs out of the round pueblo ruin. The dark vertical scar crossing the gulch is an ancient highway. Wooden beams, like those in the masonry wall opposite, were probably brought in on such roadways.

Judd already knew a great deal about the Anasazi of Chaco Canyon: that they occupied thirteen giant pueblos as well as hundreds of smaller structures in and around the canyon; that they had at least rudimentary knowledge of astronomy; and that they were skillful masons. But he had no idea how they had managed to flourish in so dry a region. He did not know why they had built curious retaining walls, or why they had carved wide, shallow depressions and stairways into the cliffs, or why, in the desert far from their pueblos, they had put up innlike wayhouses. Nor did he know why, though they lived in an arid canyon, they had laboriously built what appeared to be a system of water control, or why, having lived in the canyon from as early as A.D. 800, they quit their homes some time after A.D. 1200.

It was in the hope of answering some of these questions that Judd was excavating Pueblo Bonito, the canyon's largest ruin, on that day in the 1920's. And then, when his Navaho assistants, offering to share a secret with him, pointed out the remains of ancient roadways, the mystery of Chaco Canyon deepened. Why had the Anasazi, who had neither wheels nor draft animals, built roadways?

The roads themselves offered few clues. First of all, erosion had made them difficult to distinguish. Some ended at the canyon wall; others dwindled out in the desert. It was, in fact, a full half-century before archaeologists, using techniques Judd never dreamed of, would learn more about the highways.

It is curious that such a riddle should have come to light in Chaco Canyon, for it was, even then, one of the best-known archaeological sites in the United States. In 1849 the U.S. Army had sent Lieutenant James H. Simpson there to persuade the Navahos to behave in a more kindly manner toward the territory's farmers. He and his party named and sketched most of the

By JAMES I. EBERT *and* ROBERT K. HITCHCOCK

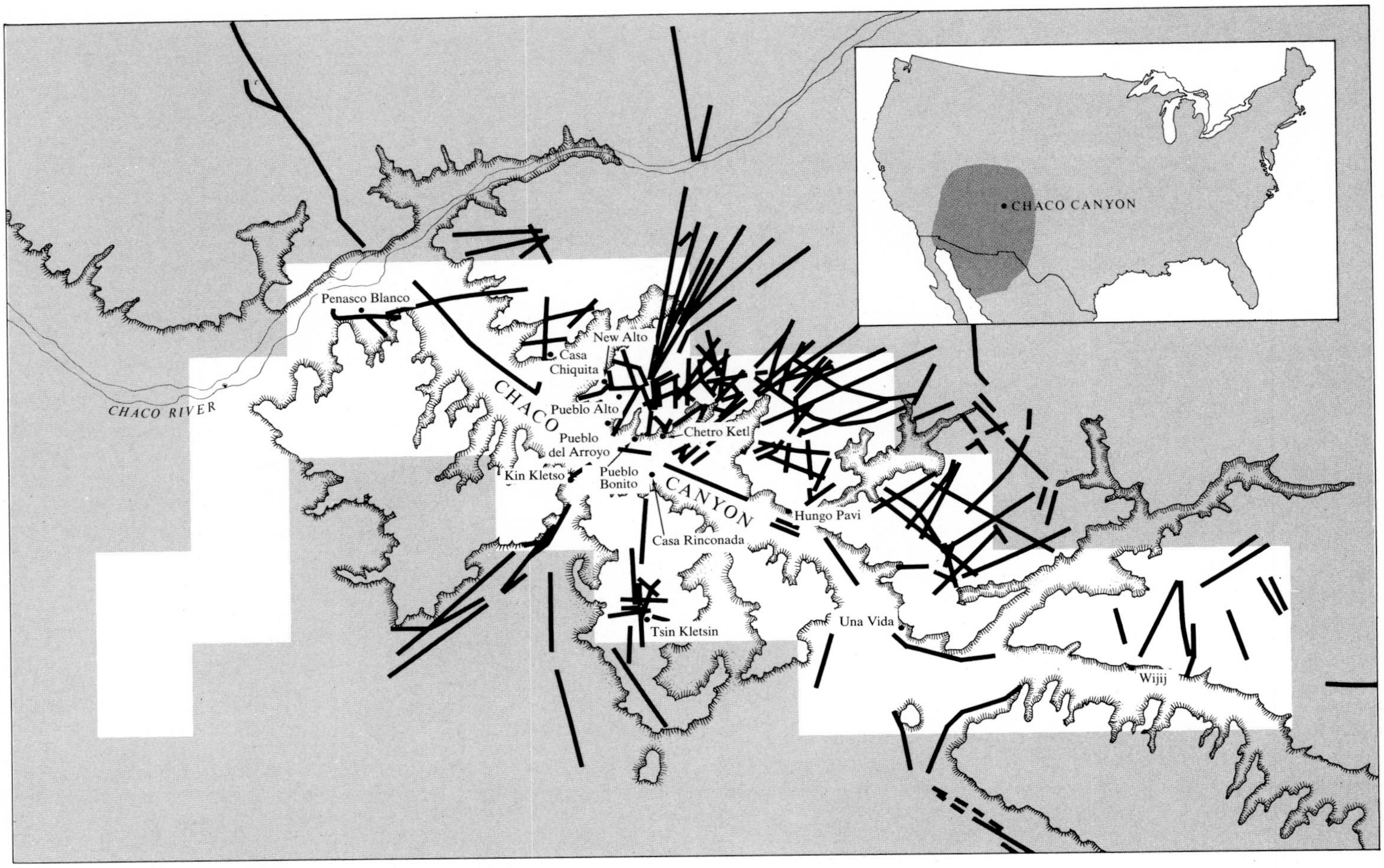

Above, a map of some of the nearly two hundred miles of ancient roads that have been discovered at Chaco Canyon. Some lead to distant Anasazi settlements; others run from pueblo to pueblo. It was an intricate system, and may have extended throughout the area indicated by the shaded part of the inset map. The light area in the large map covers the thirty-six square miles of Chaco Canyon National Monument.

canyon's major ruins, pointing the way for those who would later stream into the canyon. During the last years of the nineteenth century it was the Hyde Exploring Expedition; from 1921 to 1927, the National Geographic Society expeditions that included Neil Judd; in the 1930's and 1940's, the School of American Research and the University of Mexico; and since that time, the National Park Service, which established the Chaco Center laboratory at the University of New Mexico, where we have done a great deal of our work.

Much was learned over the years about the canyon and its early inhabitants. Archaeologists discovered, for example, that the Anasazi were neither the first nor the last people to live there. The southwestern United States may, in fact, have been occupied by man almost since his entry into the New World. Stone spear points found in the area indicate that Paleo Indian hunters were there as early as fifteen to twenty millenniums ago; nomadic gatherers of seeds and plants date from about 6000 B.C. The first settled groups, the Basketmakers, began in about A.D. 500 to live in small villages of semisubterranean pithouses and were among the first people in North America to practice agriculture. And then came the Pueblo period of the Anasazi with its multistoried, aboveground adobe and masonry dwellings, and increasing dependence on agricultural products. Thus, a thousand years ago or so, northwestern New Mexico became the scene of one of the most remarkable social and economic developments in aboriginal North America: the establishment of the great population centers of the Anasazi, of which Chaco Canyon is one of the largest.

The Anasazi, we now know, traded with the great civilizations to the south. They probably exported semiprecious stones, such as turquoise, and imported seashells, copper belts, and feathers. Studies of food remains show that they ate domesticated corn, squash, and wild seeds. They hunted deer and antelope, and probably raised turkeys.

As we have learned more about the Anasazi, we have found it increasingly difficult to view their culture in traditional ways. Prehistorians have customarily looked to the great civilizations of Central and South America for answers to questions about the ancient tribes of North America, but the Anasazi, despite their trade with cultures to the south, seem strikingly different. The ancient urban developments of Mexico occurred in areas of deep, rich soil and moderate rainfall; the Anasazi lived in an arid and unpredictable environment. Cities such as Teotihuacán and Tenochtitlán were arranged in orderly grids and compounds; Anasazi pueblos were more like giant freestanding apartment buildings. Burial customs south of the border reflect clear differences in prestige and wealth, yet the few known Anasazi burial sites show no such differences. Finally, Anasazi pottery designs often have little relationship to those of the major cultures to the south. Colin Renfrew, the English archaeologist, has concluded that the cities of the Anasazi looked more like those of Asia Minor than of Mexico.

But none of these details seemed to have any bearing on the canyon's mysterious roadways. It was not until the late 1960's that the first breakthrough occurred. While investigating Chaco Canyon's water-control system, Gwinn Vivian of the Arizona State Museum in Tucson came upon some enigmatic features that did not appear to be canals. On the mesa behind Pueblo Bonito, Vivian noticed two parallel lines of rocks that looked like the borders of a garden path. Following them, he eventually came to what was apparently a stone ramp that gave easy access to the top of a cliff. It occurred to him that many features he had previously regarded as water-control structures might instead be parts of an ancient system of roads.

Then, in 1971, archaeologists, ourselves included, discovered numerous stairways in the canyon walls. Perhaps the stairs, too, were part of a transportation system far larger than had been imagined. Checking that hunch was a problem, however, for few roads were visible from the ground. Then we recalled that aerial photographs had been taken in 1929 by none other than Charles A. Lindbergh, and decided to try again.

With aerial photography, distracting detail dissolves and points merge into lines. Shadows and differences in elevation reveal features too subtle to notice from the ground. In the case of the Chaco Canyon roadways, the results were startling. It was immediately apparent that the roads were not merely isolated avenues but part of a network of prehistoric pedestrian superhighways. One of their striking features is their straightness. Some approach a cliff face at a stairway site, then continue across the mesa at exactly the same bearing. Although most of the roads link pueblos or various gathering places, some head north, south, or east.

COURTESY UNIVERSITY OF NEW MEXICO, PUBLIC INFORMATION OFFICE

Seen from the air, Pueblo Bonito lies on the valley floor against a cliff. The largest of the pueblos, it housed some twelve hundred people in eight hundred rooms arcing around open plazas.

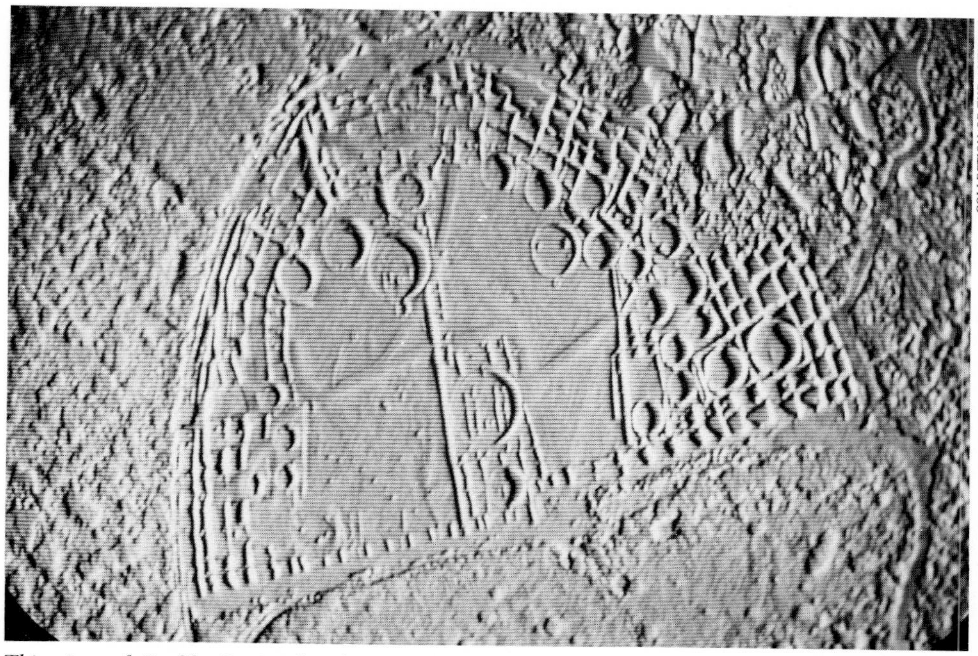

COLLECTION OF THE AUTHORS

This view of Pueblo Bonito has been interpreted electronically on the screen of the Digicol. Invented by astronomers, the device enhances faint features by deepening their shadows.

FROM JESSE D. JENNINGS, *Prehistory of North America*, MCGRAW-HILL, 1968

As here reconstructed, Pueblo Bonito rises to five stories. It is remarkably like a modern housing project and probably had the same problems—overcrowding, noise, and too much garbage.

When we had learned everything possible from studying aerial photographs with the unaided eye, we began working in the Chaco Center laboratory with the stereoscope, an instrument that uses two overlapping photographs to give a three-dimensional view. Next we turned to space-age photography and electronics. Infrared film, by showing vegetation in bright pink and red patterns, revealed several previously undiscovered stretches of road. Multispectral imaging, by photographing the same scene simultaneously with several cameras fitted with different filters, added more information on the roadway network. And the electronic Digicol, which looks like a cross between a television studio and an astronaut's instrument panel, amplified faint photographic images and thereby doubled the amount of known roadways.

Now, however, came the hard, time-consuming part—what archaeologists call gathering "ground truth." When dusty roadway segments, some of them almost thirty miles long, were walked along, measured, and photographed, several things became apparent. In almost all cases the major highways were a precise nine meters—about thirty feet—wide, and all the roads proved to have a dish-shaped cross-section. Could this have resulted from the pressure of many feet during the years they were used? If so, the contours might suggest which roads were most heavily traveled.

Ground truth also revealed that a number of Chaco Canyon's enigmas were part of the roadway network—the retaining walls, the cuts through the hills, the wayhouses in the desert. Even the function of a small section of stone wall at the bottom of a deep arroyo became clear: it served as a footbridge when the arroyo filled with water.

Thus far we have mapped a complex web of some two hundred miles of roads, some of them extending as much as sixty-five miles to connect Chaco Canyon with other major Anasazi centers. But this still does not answer the original question: why did the Anasazi, possessing neither wheeled vehicles nor beasts of burden, build roads at all?

Some archaeologists, noting that modern Pueblo Indians occasionally hold footraces, have speculated that the Anasazi roads were racetracks. Judd thought they might be ceremonial highways. But the economic pressures that almost certainly influenced the Anasazi suggest another interpretation. Consider, for example, the harsh environment in which they lived. Given our present estimates of Chaco Canyon's population a thousand years ago, perhaps as many as 15,000 inhabitants, it is almost impossible that the Anasazi could have supported themselves solely through local agriculture and hunting. Much of the food found in Chaco Canyon's mounds of trash and storage pits must have come from the hinterlands; so must the enormous ponderosa pines—as many as 100,000 of them—used in the construction of the great Anasazi pueblos. One can imagine crews of workmen carrying sixty-foot logs, some of them three feet in diameter, across mesas, down cliffs, and through arroyos in an ancient forewarning of the traffic on our own highways.

In an attempt to understand still more about the Anasazi and their roads, we have also used methods customarily employed by geographers. Today, for example, economic geographers find profitable sites for shopping centers and accurately predict traffic flows over proposed highway routes by what is called graph theory. By assigning numerical values to such things as the distance between towns, the number of connecting routes, and the economic productivity of the area under consideration, a mathematical comparison can be made with already existing transportation systems. When analyzed in this way, the Anasazi roadway network is found to be relatively "unconnected"; in other words, its component pueblos are typically connected with other pueblos only by single direct roadways. Today, similarly unconnected transport networks are characteristic of developing countries where road builders are willing to pay initial high costs to ensure that future travel

The Anasazi at Home

The everyday objects of the Anasazi are both well-made and handsome. In earliest times, after 100 B.C., they used baskets for cooking as well as carrying. Later they began to make pots that resembled baskets, to paint crisp, black-on-white, geometric designs, and to use imaginative forms—such as the duck-shaped pitcher below.

Basket

Basketlike pot

Striped straw sandal

Pitcher

Jet and turquoise frog

is cheap and efficient. The engineering efforts of the Anasazi could hardly have been justified if casual foot travel was the only use foreseen for Anasazi roads. When the vast road system was built, the Anasazi were looking forward primarily to the long-distance transport of heavy goods—goods borne by humans.

No doubt there was an ever-increasing demand for imported necessities following the population explosion that began after A.D. 800. The Anasazi may have withstood the strain for a while by farming, irrigating, and hunting more intensively. But then, inevitably, an insupportable depletion of resources would have occurred. (Archaeologists investigating an agricultural area in the canyon in 1974, for example, found hard-packed soil and an accumulation of salts that indicate overfarming.) Only then, perhaps, as the Anasazi sought to extend their vast highway system in search of more food, did it become apparent that their self-sufficiency had been stretched dangerously thin, and that they were vulnerable to internal and external pressures.

In the end, it is more than likely that civil conflict speeded Chaco Canyon's decline and abandonment. If, as we suspect, there were no public officials, political and economic power was probably held by people who rose, not through heredity, but through personal popularity or their ability to extend loans. In such a society rivalries are invariably intense. If, as some have suggested, the Chaco Canyon road system was privately owned, then a few people, for some reason disgruntled and looking for revenge, could have curtailed the flow of food, fuel, and building materials.

Whatever happened at Chaco Canyon, its great pueblos saw fewer inhabitants and less trade after 1175. By 1250 the sandstone walls that once rang with the sounds of a complex civilization had fallen silent.

James Ebert and Robert Hitchcock spent two years working in Chaco Canyon. They will study the Bushmen of Botswana for a year before completing their doctorates.

AMERICAN MUSEUM OF NATURAL HISTORY

Chaco Canyon has been under investigation since the last century. Above, Indians excavate Pueblo Bonito in 1897. Below are the ruins of Chetro Ketl. Though aware of the canyon's ancient highways, the Indians did not point them out to archaeologists until the 1920's.

J. BRYAN

THE MAKING OF A HERETIC

For eight years Church authorities searched for a reason not to burn this quarrelsome, opinionated, and altogether brilliant troublemaker. In the end, he left them no choice

The year 1600 was to be a Holy Year, a year of universal jubilee. As their ancestors had done for the first Christian jubilee three centuries before, tens of thousands of pilgrims would flock to Rome. Traditionally the celebration began on Christmas Eve, when the Porta Santa of St. Peter's basilica, sealed at the close of the previous jubilee, was reopened by the pope. But on Christmas Eve, 1599, Clement VIII was confined to his bed with a severe case of gout, and the ceremony had to be postponed until December 31.

At six o'clock that evening, the pope, though still not well, was carried through the crowds massed before St. Peter's to the steps of the basilica. While the Swiss Guards beat back the pilgrims with their staves, the papal chair was lowered to the ground and the Supreme Pontiff helped to his feet. Taking little mincing steps and being careful not to bend his swollen knees, Clement eventually reached the Porta Santa, where he was handed a gilded hammer with which he struck the holy door three times. At the third stroke assistants removed the enclosing wall. Ignoring the excruciating pain the gesture must have cost him, the sixty-four-year-old pontiff sank to his knees to intone the Te Deum. During this Holy Year, he appeared determined to set the world an example of piety and self-abnegation.

On February 12 the Fuggers' correspondent reported that Clement had ordered all carpets and ornaments removed from his rooms, as he wished "only to be between four walls." That same day, the *avvisi*, or public notices, announced that "solemn justice" would be done upon a Dominican friar of Nola, "a most obstinate heretic." His name was Giordano Bruno. If God did not help him, the "wretch" was to be burned alive.

BRITISH MUSEUM, PRINTS AND DRAWINGS DEPARTMENT

Bruno, in a nineteenth-century engraving

An auto-da-fé was no ordinary execution; it was an important religious event. Notices were read in all the churches, requesting the pilgrims to attend. The Holy Father, they were told, wished that this awesome spectacle, coming as it did at the commencement of the jubilee year, should illustrate to the world how heretics were treated in Rome. The execution was to occur on Friday, February 17, in the Campo dei Fiori.

At six o'clock that morning, four members of the confraternity of St. John the Beheaded, clad in the black cassocks of their order and carrying lanterns and placards painted with scenes from the Passion, proceeded through the dark, chilly streets to the prison of the Tor di Nona near the Tiber. There they were introduced to the condemned man. Holding scenes of the Passion before his eyes, they pleaded with him to recant. When their efforts failed, they called for reinforcements. Since the condemned man was a Dominican and a doctor of theology, it seemed only natural to summon priests well-versed in canon law. But though these learned men sought to prove to the prisoner the error of his thinking, he persisted in what would later be described as his "cursed obstinacy." Refusing to be discouraged, the fathers continued to remonstrate with him until the minister of justice arrived to conduct him to the stake.

Even then the members of the company of St. John and the others did not desert him. During the long march from the Tor di Nona they walked beside him, chanting litanies, urging him to kiss the painted tablets of the Crucifixion, pointing out his errors, and beseeching him to recant. But he ignored them, treating them like so many flies buzzing about his head and turning away from which-

By RACHEL ERLANGER

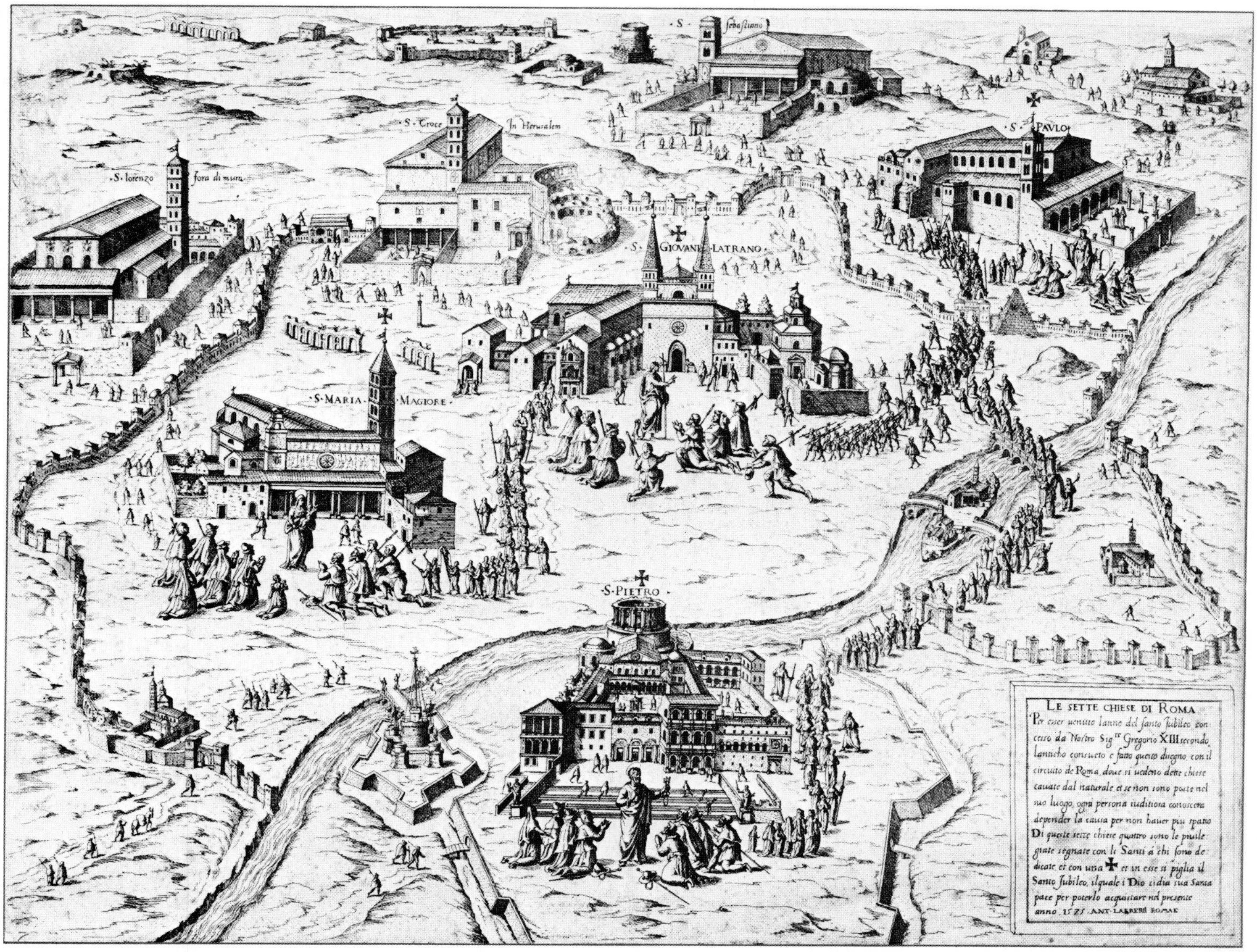

The seven basilicas of Rome appear on a pilgrims' guide for the 1575 jubilee. The dome of St. Peter's (foreground) was not completed until 1590.

GABINETTO NAZIONALE DELLE STAMPE

ever friar happened to be reasoning with him at the moment.

He was a thin, frail-looking man of fifty-two, neither handsome nor ugly, with dark brown hair, a sparse black beard, and the livid, unhealthy complexion that comes from long years in prison. His feet were bare and his only piece of clothing was a sulfurous yellow penitent's shirt painted with flames, devils, and a cross of Saint Andrew. As he came into view many members of the waiting crowd averted their gaze lest he give them the evil eye.

At the Campo dei Fiori he was stripped. A wedge was stuck in his mouth to keep him from uttering blasphemies as he died, and his nude body was bound to the stake. Once more the priests implored him to recant; once more he refused. Motioning for the crowd to stand back, the executioner applied a lighted torch to the pile of twigs and straw. A few of the spectators looked away, but most watched in greedy silence. Often, when a heretic felt the fire touch his body, weird subhuman moans could be heard forcing their way past the obstruction to his tongue. But Bruno remained impassive—further proof, if any were needed, that he was possessed by the devil. At the last moment the unhappy prisoner was offered a crucifix to gaze upon as he died. He rejected it with a wild and disdainful look. The orange flames spluttered and crackled, then turned a blinding yellow, and the acrid smell of burning flesh filled the morning air. Led by the friars, the vast crowd burst into song: "Great God, we praise Thee."

That afternoon, as Bruno's books were burned before the steps of the basilica in St. Peter's Square, few must have bothered to glance at the titles: *On the Infinite Universe and Worlds*; *Of the Cause, Principles and Unity*. Certainly, none could have had any idea how much those works would influence future generations of philosophers and writers, from Spinoza to Leibnitz to James Joyce.

Given Bruno's tactless and impetuous nature and his propensity to question all things, he picked an inopportune time to be born. By that year, 1548, the golden days of the Renaissance were over; in 1543 Paul III revived the Roman Inquisition; in 1545 the conservative Council of Trent met for the first time. "Better to reason as little as possible," said a pasquinade written soon afterward.

In the bright morning of Bruno's life, there was no hint of the agony to come. Nola, his birthplace, is an ancient, walled, southern Italian city surrounded by tree-covered mountains and green fields planted with row after row of espaliered grapevines. Years later, when far from home, he would come to feel that all that was good in this world was concentrated in that lovely countryside.

When Bruno was eleven his father sent him to study in Naples. His principal tutor was an Augustinian friar, Fra Teofilo de Vairano, who taught him logic and Aristotelian metaphysics. When he was about fifteen, he enrolled in the public classes of the Studium Generale, or University of Naples, which in those days were held in the courtyard of San Domenico.

In the lovely old courtyard, fragrant with the smell of citrus blossoms, he heard the sixteenth-century followers of Saint Thomas Aquinas, the fathers of San Domenico, disputing questions of doctrine with unruly students. In 1565, when he was seventeen years old, his admiration for the Dominicans led him to become a novice in the cloister of San Domenico—or so he would one day tell a fellow prisoner of the Inquisition.

During Bruno's first year at San Domenico, he appears to have been too enraptured by the prospect of serving God to question anything. His probation over, he took his vows of poverty, chastity, and obedience, discarded his baptismal name, Filippo, and was rechristened Giordano after the river Jordan.

Not long afterward, the first signs of rebellion appeared. One day he disposed of the images of the saints in his cell, keeping only the crucifix. Coming upon one of his fellow novices reading *The Seven Joys of the Madonna*, an insipid religious work of the time, Bruno demanded to know why the boy wasn't reading a more worthwhile book. The boy immediately reported the conversation to the master of the novices. The master did not, however, take the incident very seriously, merely writing a memorandum of what had happened and warning his young charge to be more careful in the future. That Bruno's behavior was the outward manifestation of an intense inner struggle apparently never occurred to him.

From his eighteenth year, as Bruno would later tell the judges of the Inquisition, he had doubted the doctrine of the Trinity. Nor was this all. His irrevocable vow of chastity, he now concluded, was "unreasonable and unnatural." He was young, he was passionate; why curb his perfectly natural instincts? Other aspects of monastic life also began to rankle. The fathers, who from afar had seemed such "godlike" men, on closer acquaintance proved to be "asses." Always a brilliant student, he had been assigned to the school of sacred theology at the university. Now he found himself less and less inclined to accept what he considered to be the dogmatic and ignorant pronouncements of his instructors. One day while playing a word game he came upon a quotation from the poet Ariosto: *"Di ogni legge nemico et di ogni fede."* (Of every law an enemy and of every faith.) The quotation suited his mood. Henceforth, he would question all things.

There was, for example, the matter of Aristotle. Though the Dominicans considered Aristotle's theories virtually the same as divine law, Bruno soon found himself rejecting Aristotle and instead turning for guidance to less orthodox sources such as the Roman Lucretius. Whereas Aristotle declared that outside this world there is nothing, not even empty space, Lucretius described the universe as infinite. The trouble was that the Church considered Lucretius an atheist, since the earth-centered universe of Aristotle was more consonant with Christian dogma.

In that compact little universe the earth was a motionless sphere around which the sun and the planets rotated in perfect circles. Beyond these planetary spheres was the sphere of the fixed stars and beyond that the sphere of the Prime Mover, who was God. To eliminate the discrepancies between Aristotle's system and the observed movements of the planets, Claudius Ptolemy, a second-century Greek astronomer living in Alexandria, gave each planet an epicycle in which it moved while traversing the rim of its perfect circle.

In the *De revolutionibus orbium* Copernicus eliminated these epicycles and had the earth and the six known planets revolve about the sun. The so-called fixed stars remained in the eighth sphere, where Aristotle had placed them. Whether this was the extent of the universe Copernicus did not say. Bruno, reading the Polish astronomer with a bias that came from having read Lucretius, concluded that it wasn't. Aristotle had justified the small size of the universe by the necessity of the heavens' turning around the earth once each day. But if, as Copernicus had demonstrated, the fixed stars did not in fact turn around the earth, Bruno could see no need for them to huddle together in the eighth sphere. Instead, he pictured them as extending out in all directions, in which case the sun and its planets became one of an endless number of solar systems drifting in an infinite universe.

Though it seems the logical deduction to have made from the Copernican data, no one else in Europe had as yet made it, possibly because of fear of Church censure, possibly because of lack of interest. Commenting upon the disparity between the Aristotelian and the Copernican theories, Montaigne demanded to know what moral he was to deduce, "unless that we should not bother which of the two is so."

Bruno was incapable of such nonchalance. The young monk, physically and mentally circumscribed by the rules of the grim order to which he had sworn allegiance, exulted in the idea of those limitless spaces. By this time, in fact, his mind had become a Pandora's box of heretical opinions. If any one of them was openly acknowledged, it could destroy him. Bruno was ingenuous enough, however, to believe that he had only to present his ideas in a sufficiently convincing manner for others to find them as irresistible as he did. Nor could he overcome the temptation to argue and explain. Once launched upon a tirade, he found himself carried along on the current of his own invective. The outburst over, he promptly forgot about it.

Surprisingly enough, Bruno managed to escape censure for ten years. Then one day, the cloister had a visitor, Fra Agostino di Montecalcino, a well-known scholar and an admirer of that rigid school of theology made famous by Torquemada, the Spanish Grand Inquisitor. In the course of a discussion with the distinguished guest, Bruno defended the followers of Arius, a second-century heretic who had questioned the validity of the Trinity. That afternoon Fra Agostino reported what he had heard to Fra Domenico Vita, the provincial of the Dominican order. Fra Domenico acted at once. He exhumed the old charges against Bruno, interviewed a number of the friars with whom he had discussed his ideas, and drew up a list of thirty-six charges of heresy. Bruno, warned by friends of what was happening, fled along the Appian Way to Rome.

After a brief stay in the Holy City, he wandered north, earning a living by teaching and writing. It is perhaps indicative of Bruno's confusion that, despite his rupture with the Church, he depended mainly on the Dominicans for food and shelter. Eventually, after drifting aimlessly from cloister to cloister, he crossed the Alps and took shelter in a cloister near Chambéry. There an Italian friar warned him that it would be safer for him to abandon his monastic robes and go to Geneva.

The Church of Calvin, he soon discovered, was no more tolerant of dissent than the Church of Rome. Three months after his enrollment as a student at the University of Geneva, he was arrested for publishing an attack against Antoine de la Faye, one of the most influential Aristotelians on the faculty. Only after he agreed to tear up his denunciation and apologize to the professor was he allowed to go free. He quit the city soon afterward.

Lyon, Toulouse, Paris, London, Oxford, Marburg, Wittenberg, Prague, Helmstedt, Frankfurt—the story of the next sixteen years is the story of his unceasing efforts to spread his version of the Copernican theory, "to make the knowledge of an infinite universe known to everyone, to prove the composition of other worlds the same as this." No sooner would he arrive in a new city or town than he would seek permission to lecture there, usually to the students at the university. The lectures, like the many books he wrote during those years, were amalgams of wildly disparate elements. On the one hand there was a poetic fervor, a sense of mission, a desire to share his own exultation with his audience. On the other there was an unbridled penchant for verbal abuse, a frantic contempt for the supporters of Aristotle.

He seldom knew when to stop. Once in a fit of pique he told an audience that Aristotle was the stupidest of all philosophers and had probably been reincarnated as a pig. At Oxford the commotion he caused resulted in the cancellation of his public lectures. At the College of Cambrai outside Paris he needed all his ingenuity to escape unharmed after a young Parisian lawyer so effectively refuted his arguments that the students turned upon Bruno and demanded an apology.

In addition to his ceaseless championing of the Copernican system during those years, Bruno also devoted much time to the works of Raymond Lull, a thirteenth-century Catalan monk who had developed an elaborate memory-improvement system that relied on strange symbols and intricate mnemonic devices. Though Bruno's numerous books on the Lullian system have led some to conclude that he was more magician than philosopher, it seems logical to see them as one thread in a complex tapestry. Far more interesting, and far more readable, are the dialogues in which he sought a metaphys in harmony with his new cosmology.

Dante and the theologians of the Middle Ages had pictured heaven as an immovable tenth sphere, or Empyrean, where, in a light that no one could

Copernicus, by an anonymous artist

The Infinite Universe

Nicolaus Copernicus revolutionized astronomy—and the future of all science—in 1543, when he published his *De revolutionibus orbium coelestium.* Though he saw a finished copy of the book only on his deathbed, he paved the way for Bruno, Galileo, Kepler, and countless others, for in one stroke he set the sun squarely at the center of the universe. In doing so, he demolished the ancient Aristotelian-Ptolemaic belief that the earth was the center around which all else revolved.

Though the first edition of *De revolutionibus* contained a preface—written by Andreas Osiander, and included without Copernicus's knowledge—warning readers that the theory was not to be taken seriously, the system gradually became known on the Continent and in England. When Bruno encountered Copernicus's book, it was a revelation to him. He then transformed the work of "this important, subtle, diligent, and mature mind," as he later wrote, into a completely new cosmology. Though Copernicus had retained the notion of an eighth sphere of fixed stars, Bruno went one step further: he extended the stars in all directions, and was the first to envision an infinite universe.

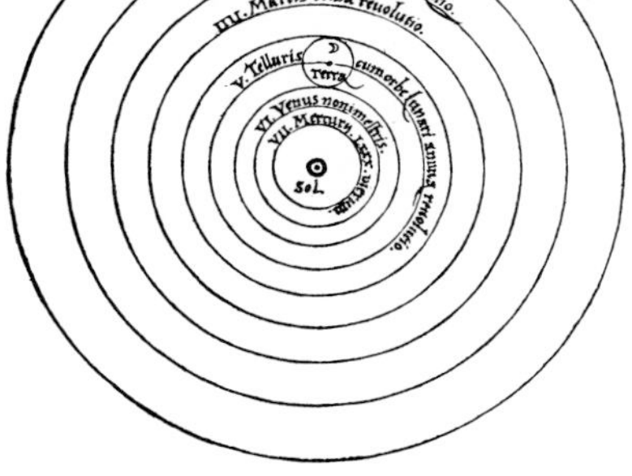

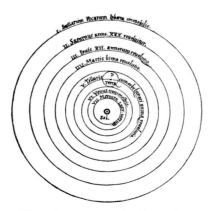

The universe as seen by Copernicus

enter, the tripartite God of Christian dogma sat enthroned. But if the universe was infinite, and there was no tenth sphere, where was God? In a conception of the Deity that owed a little to Pythagoras, a little to Plato's *Timaeus*, and a little to the Egyptian Neoplatonist Plotinus, Bruno replaced the anthropomorphic extramundane God of Judaeo-Christian theology with an immanent God—"the soul of the universe, nature revealed, a being who comprises all things, who is the fountain of all being, in whom exists everything that is."

Given such a concept of the Deity, the Trinity appears superfluous, nor does humankind need elaborate rituals and the intervention of priests. Discussing the myth of Actaeon, Bruno has the poet Tansillo say: "Now that he had compressed divinity into himself, there was no longer any occasion to hunt for it elsewhere."

In his concept of an inner God, Bruno saw the basis for a universal nondogmatic faith that would replace the old outmoded creeds and solve the pointless quarrels that were decimating Europe. But though at times he seems to have actively sought converts, whom he called *giordanista*, he never seemed able to establish clearly in his own mind the relationship between this new religion and the Church he had once loved so dearly.

Somewhere in Bruno's mind lurked the conviction that if only the right people in the Church's hierarchy heard of his ideas, they would accept them. During his wanderings through northern Europe the hope of a reconciliation with the Church recurs like a leitmotif. While in Paris, he sought to have the papal nuncio discuss with the pope the question of absolution. Since the nuncio was convinced that Sixtus V would not even hear the plea unless Bruno returned to his order, the matter was dropped.

In 1590, while Bruno was in Frankfurt, one of his books on memory improvement attracted the attention of Giovanni Mocenigo, a wealthy Venetian nobleman. As a youth Mocenigo had studied architecture but had later abandoned that profession for literature. To shine in the world of belles-lettres, to dazzle the intelligentsia with his wit and erudition, became his one desire. But how accomplish this when one's memory was bad and one had not read very much? Bruno's book seemed to Mocenigo the answer, and he invited Giordano to become his private tutor. Bruno, who was then forty-two years of age and had been wandering from place to place for sixteen years, accepted.

Those who knew him found the decision incomprehensible. Over and over again he had denounced the Inquisition, the "open jaw of the Roman wolf," and had predicted that if he ever strayed into Roman Catholic lands a hundred, nay a thousand, torches would light him to his grave. Once having made up his mind to return to Italy, however, he found innumerable arguments to justify his decision. He was going not to Rome, after all, but to Venice, where the Inquisition was the mildest in Italy. The times, in any event, appeared propitious. Gregory XIV, a man as mild as Sixtus had been stern,

Galileo vs. the Inquisition

LOUVRE, CABINET DES DESSINS

Galileo Galilei in 1624

Bruno's execution in 1600 was intended by the Inquisition to put an end to science and to discourage incipient heretics like Galileo. In 1597 he had written Johannes Kepler, "Like you I accepted the Copernican position years ago."

Galileo's belief was known to only a few colleagues, yet he could not remain silent. His discovery of Jupiter's satellites in 1611 was proof, as Jacob Bronowski has written, "that the Ptolemaic heaven simply would not work." And in 1613 Galileo openly admitted his Copernican belief. Soon after, he was denounced before the Inquisition.

Galileo had a fatal flaw: he thought he merely had to demonstrate that Copernicus was right and everybody would listen. But he had not reckoned on Robert Bellarmine, S.J., a man sympathetic to new ideas yet unable to reconcile his orthodox beliefs with scientific notions that threatened the Church's position. He had quizzed Bruno in 1600; in 1616 he confronted Galileo.

Galileo understood from Bellarmine—and had a signed document for proof—that while the Copernican system could not be defended as fact, it could be used as a hypothesis. This is what Galileo did in *Dialogue on the Great World Systems*, published in 1632.

The next year, he was again called before the Inquisition, where officials produced another document—undated, unsigned—saying Galileo had been prohibited from teaching the Copernican theory in any form, even as a hypothesis. Confronted with this "evidence" and threatened with torture, Galileo recanted and was forced to retire in silence to a villa near Florence. Four years later he went blind, and in 1642 he died.

BIBLIOTHEQUE NATIONALE

Above: Robert Bellarmine; below: the forged document used against Galileo

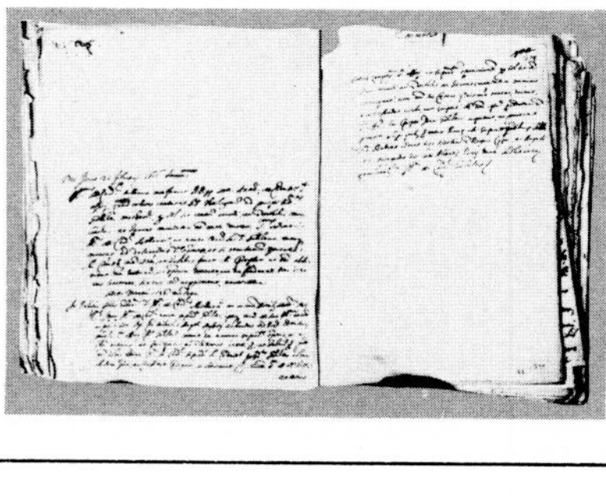

ARCHIVIO SEGRETO VATICANO

BIBLIOTHEQUE NATIONALE — GIRAUDON

A suspected heretic is quizzed by a high official of the Inquisition while a scribe (left) records the testimony.

was now pope. Surely this was the moment to attempt the long-deferred reconciliation with the Church.

During Bruno's first months in Venice his optimism seemed justified. He was allowed to lecture at the nearby University of Padua. His patron appeared to be satisfied with what he was learning, so satisfied that he invited his teacher to move into the Casa Mocenigo. Though Bruno must have realized his host's intellectual limitations soon enough, he seems to have had no misgivings. Not only did he move into Mocenigo's palace, he also allowed his pupil to question him on a number of subjects besides the art of memory.

Had he, a monk, known women?
To the extent of his opportunity, though he had not yet reached Solomon's number.
What did he think of the friars?
All friars were asses. They should be made to live on broth as in France.
How did he feel about the Church?
Truly, the Catholic Church pleased him more than any of the others, but it was in need of great reform.

These unorthodox opinions, coupled as they were with his pronouncements concerning the infinity of the universe, gradually convinced Mocenigo that he was dealing with a man possessed by the devil. Had he been learning anything he considered of value, he might have overlooked this disturbing fact. But after seven months of study with Bruno, Mocenigo could not detect the slightest improvement in his memory.

When Bruno announced he was returning to Frankfurt, Mocenigo began to think of how he might best revenge himself on his recalcitrant teacher. Unable to bear the thought of all the money he had wasted on lessons, Mocenigo decided to make one last attempt to wrest the mystery of memory from his teacher, this time menacing him with the Holy Inquisition. Bruno ignored the threats. On the very next night Mocenigo arranged to have him imprisoned in a garret of his palace. From there he was transferred to San Domenico di Castello, the Inquisition stronghold. On May 25, 1592, his trial for heresy began.

As was so often the case in such trials, the question of an actual crime was not even discussed. Instead the judges sought to penetrate the mind of the accused, to determine whether his thinking had strayed from orthodoxy. Like most inquisitors, they were carefully trained jurists and theologians who made an honest effort to conduct what they considered a fair trial.

But though they allowed the prisoner to explain his beliefs at great length, the inquisitors never really heard what he had to say. Nor were they interested in hearing him. All they wanted to know was how many heretical views the accused admitted to holding. Could he be persuaded to recant?

No sooner had Bruno finished outlining the principles of his philosophy than the Father Inquisitor commenced a staccato cross-examination based upon the accusations submitted by Mocenigo. Under this barrage of questions Bruno's self-confidence crumbled. He had hoped to be judged upon the substance of his philosophy. The little heresies he had uttered from time to time he considered unimportant. But to the inquisitors all heresies were equally significant. Half-forgotten outbursts directed at Mocenigo, words written years ago in the safety of England, even jokes and idle boasts—all these incautious opinions now formed part of the case amassed against him. He had denied the existence of the Trinity. He had eaten meat on fast days. He had praised England's renegade Queen Elizabeth. The sheer number of the heretical statements he had made during his forty-four years overwhelmed him. No explanation could possibly wipe them away.

The more clearly Bruno realized this, the more frantic became his efforts to conciliate his judges. Gone was the dignity of his earlier testimony. He lied; he contradicted himself; he resorted to histrionics. Finally, after a prolonged cross-examination concerning his views about "the sin of the flesh outside matrimony," the utter hopelessness of his position must have become all too apparent, for he seems to have broken down completely.

WEIDENFELD AND NICOLSON ARCHIVES

Stubborn heretics were persuaded to confess by being stretched on the rack or suspended from a cord.

After that he was not examined for almost seven weeks. And when, on July 30, he was again summoned before the Holy Tribunal, not a trace of the hellfire that had once so provoked his audiences survived. Falling to his knees, he asked pardon of God and the inquisitors for the errors he had committed. He promised his judges that if they granted him his life, he would reform and make recompense for the scandal he had caused.

"Do you have anything else to say?" the Father Inquisitor asked.

"No, nothing else," Bruno replied.

His answer was accepted; he was returned to his cell and the court was adjourned. The trial had ended.

The Venetian trial, however, was only the first act. Inquisitorial procedure demanded that before sentence be passed upon any prisoner, a report of his case must be forwarded to Rome. A little more than a month after receipt of the document, Cardinal Santaseverina, one of the nine inquisitors, officially requested that the accused be surrendered to Rome for further questioning.

On February 27, 1593, Bruno entered the Fabbrica Grande, the vast and gloomy inquisitorial jail between the Tiber and the Vatican. In the end, he was to spend seven years in that Roman dungeon, during which he sought the courage to stand by his convictions while the Inquisition, if we are to judge by the records, sought the courage to burn him.

He had endless time to think during those seven years. When, a few months after his incarceration, officials of the Holy Office began cross-examining him, the servile creature who had fallen to his knees and begged the court of Venice for mercy no longer existed. The long months in jail had blunted the sharp edge of his terror; now he appeared eager to salvage at least some of his ideas. Confronted with a list of twenty-four heresies, Bruno would agree to renounce one, only to reiterate it more forcefully at a later interrogation.

The men sent to question him were Dominican priests like himself. Accuser and accused had attended the same schools; both sides knew the same arguments; both could quote the same sources. For an entire year the assessor and the Father Commissary of the Holy Office debated doctrine with the prisoner. Eventually, however, the Sisyphean nature of their task must have become all too apparent. At the end of March, 1597, the court noted that Bruno was subjected to the usual half-hour application of the cord. Stretched on the rack, suspended by the cord, he still refused to change his views. What was one to do with such an exasperating prisoner? Nothing remained but to sentence him. Once more he was left alone in his cell—this time for almost a year—while the Holy Office considered its verdict.

Now the last of the principal players in this bitter farce took his place at stage center. He was Cardinal Robert Bellarmine, a Jesuit who had recently been appointed to both the College of Cardinals and the Holy Tribunal. The author of *Controversies*, an ecclesiastical best seller, and master of controversial questions for the Jesuits, His Eminence had spent his entire life in theological debate. Furthermore, while still a bishop Bellarmine had helped catalogue the errors in Bruno's books.

Bellarmine's native common sense told him that it was useless to dicker over evidence. The situation demanded a show of strength. Rather than present the accused with the lengthy and admittedly controversial summary that had been prepared, His Eminence offered to draw up a list of incontrovertibly erroneous doctrines extracted from it. Upon these the prisoner would be denied all possibility of equivocation. Either he abjured them or he would be sentenced as a heretic. Since, moreover, he had already recanted once in Venice, a refusal to recant would make him a heretic *relapsus*. For such equivocators the stake was inevitable.

Two days after the cardinals accepted Bellarmine's offer, he submitted eight propositions to them. Exactly what they were is not known, but the way they were used reveals the mutual desperation of accuser and accused.

Faced with a choice between renouncing his ideas and being burnt at the stake, Bruno indicated his willingness to renounce the eight propositions, but even as the Father Inquisitor was drawing up a suitable "act of faith" for him to sign, the prisoner began to have second thoughts. In March he dispatched a letter to Cardinal Bellarmine which, though it still indicated a desire to recant, did not sound as unequivocal as his previous statement. On September 9, when he appeared before the inquisitors, he once again expressed a willingness to recant. No sooner did he return to his cell, however, than he dispatched a letter to the pope explaining his position.

The exasperated inquisitors gave him forty days to reconsider. The forty days stretched to eighty, but still the prisoner showed not the slightest inclination to renounce his opinions. When at the end of those eighty days of solitary confinement the door of his cell opened to admit Father Hippolytus Maria Beccaria, director-general of the Dominican order, and his vicar, Paolo dello Mirandola, Bruno informed them that their visit was in vain. He ought not recant; he had nothing to recant; he would not recant.

From being on the defensive and seeking to appease his judges, he had abruptly shifted to the offensive. Suddenly it had come to him that these priests had no right to question him this way, and that in truth there was nothing for him to recant and there never had been. And though he was still in chains in his gloomy windowless cell in the Fabbrica Grande, the realization made him free, for now at last he had broken the remaining links that bound him to the Church. After months of turmoil, the man and his beliefs had coalesced. At long last he understood that the words he had written so many years before were not merely empty words, that his responsibility to that inner God he had once declared lives in every man, "nearer to him than his own soul," made capitulation to these niggling priests impossible. And this responsibility to his own ideas is the real meaning of his life.

Clement VIII, above, became pope in 1592, the year Bruno's heresy trial began in Venice.

On January 20, 1600, Bruno's refusal to recant was duly reported to the pope. He also received another letter from Bruno, seeking to justify his behavior. His Holiness opened the letter but, according to the papal notary, did not read it. Doubtless the pontiff had by then tired of this stubborn friar and his endless explanatory epistles. After listening to the reports of his cardinals, Clement directed that they make arrangements to sentence the prisoner.

Three weeks later, in the palace of the Grand Inquisitor, the sentencing took place. The soldiers made the condemned kneel for the reading—a tiny figure surrounded by hostile priests. The verdict was as follows:

> We declare you, Fra Giordano Bruno, an impenitent and pertinacious heretic . . . and we drive you forth from . . . our holy and immaculate church of whose mercy you have become unworthy . . . and surrender you to the authority of the governor of Rome. . . .

No sooner had the notary read the names of the nine cardinal inquisitors who had signed the document than the despised figure rose to address his judges. "You who convict me show greater fear than I who hear myself condemned," he told them.

In the excitement of the jubilee year the execution was soon forgotten. Later that February the pope, assisted by Cardinal Bellarmine, celebrated mass in the great vaulted church of the Gesù. During Holy Week the pontiff seated himself in the chair of the grand penitentiary in St. Peter's and, emulating a simple parish priest, heard confession for hours on end. In his *History of the Popes* Baron Pastor describes the amazement of the Protestants who were in Rome:

> They saw with their own eyes the Pope assiduously visiting the churches and imitating the true servant of God, the humble actions of the Saviour and washing and kissing the feet of the pilgrims; how he furnished the needy with money, waited upon the sick, consoled everyone.

As always, the Holy Father tried to do what was right, confident that history would one day include him among the great vicars of his Church. How could he know that the ideas of that miserable heretic who had burned to death in the Campo dei Fiori, and of his mentor Copernicus, would destroy the world in which all that piety, all that kissing of pilgrims' feet, was taken seriously. How could he know that when future generations remembered the reign of Clement VIII it would be for what he had done to a wicked, blaspheming friar whose name he would perhaps have been hard put to remember.

Rachel Erlanger became interested in Bruno during a stay in Italy. This article is based on part of a book she is currently writing on Counter Reformation Rome.

JIM AND PHYLLIS

1
Jim Barnstable was a clerk in a savings bank.
2
PARIS
Phyllis Woodson was working in a travel agency. But she never travel-led.
3
He lived in a hotel room. He had a color T.V.
4
She rented a room in the apartment of an old lady.
5
They met in a coffee shop on a Sunday night. He made a joke because they had ordered exactly the same things (a cheeseburger and a glass of milk).
6
A few months later they got mar-ried.

A LOVE STORY

A story by Pierre le-Tan

7
They bought a house in a suburb.
8
They didn't have any children. They had a peaceful life.
9
Every Sunday they would take a drive in the neighborhood.
10
For the seventh anniversary of their marriage Jim gave a cat to Phyllis.
11
One day he drowned himself in a swamp.
12
CHEZ PHYLLIS
Phyllis sold the house and opened a topless bar in an industrial area.

PRINCE OF PAINTERS

Thus did an English patron describe Peter Paul Rubens, who, with characteristic self-confidence, once wrote: "My endowments are such that my courage has always been equal to any enterprise"

By J. H. ELLIOTT

LOUVRE—ARCHIVES PHOTOGRAPHIQUES

ABOVE: *A self-portrait of the artist in his late fifties.* OPPOSITE: THE MAJORITY OF LOUIS XIII, 1623–1625. *The French ship of state, as Rubens conceived it, fairly pulsates with feminine energy. The craft is powered by four husky oarswomen, and it is piloted by the torch-bearing figure of France herself. At left, a youthful Louis XIII takes the tiller from his mother, Marie de Médicis.*

ALTE PINAKOTHEK, MUNICH

The Artist and His Wife Isabella Brandt in the Honeysuckle Bower, 1609

In a world torn by violence and fanaticism and social conflict, one could do worse than heed the following advice: "We are living in a time when life itself is possible only if one frees oneself of every burden, like a swimmer in a stormy sea." These words were written in London three and a half centuries ago by a man who well knew the dangers he faced. For few seas, before or since, have been stormier than those that threatened to engulf Europe in the early seventeenth century, and if anyone had a chance of swimming safely to shore, it was the author of that excellent advice: Europe's most famous living painter, Peter Paul Rubens.

No doubt there was an element of luck in Rubens's career, but no man worked harder to command good fortune and no man deserved it more. Endowed with an extraordinary range of gifts, Rubens not only perfected them by sheer hard work but integrated them into a well-balanced whole, with the result that of all his works of art, perhaps the greatest was his own personality. His superabundant energy could so easily have been dissipated, his fluency could so easily have degenerated into mere facility, his amiability into empty charm. As it was, Rubens's strength of character enabled him to impose his own terms on the world, a world much in need of what he had to offer: humanity, a sense of proportion, an inner peace.

With its religious divisions and periodic outbursts of violence, the Netherlands in the latter half of the sixteenth century was a microcosm of Europe. In 1567 the duke of Alba marched north from Milan at the head of a Spanish army to reimpose order on Philip II's rebellious Low Country provinces, where aristocratic opposition and religious unrest had made common cause against his regime. "Order" was restored, at least temporarily, but at the price of a mass migration of some of the most vigorous elements in Netherlands society—townspeople profoundly unsympathetic to the constricting Counter Reformation Catholicism that Spain was attempting to impose by force.

One of these émigrés was Rubens's father, Jan, a cultivated and debonair lawyer. Because his flirtation with Calvinist doctrines suggested the wisdom of a temporary absence from his native Antwerp, he and his wife Maria and their children settled in Cologne. There he became first the secretary and then the secret lover of Anne of Saxony, the wife of Prince William of Orange, the leader of the Dutch resistance to Spain. The eventual discovery of Jan's relationship with the princess brought imprisonment and the threat of a death sentence, but he won reprieve and release through the efforts of Maria, a woman whose determination and steadfastness contrasted sharply with the fickle charm of her husband. After Jan's release, two more children were born: Philip, who in due course became a distinguished humanist scholar and secretary to the city of Antwerp, and, in 1577, Peter Paul. Ten years later Jan Rubens died, and Maria, now restored to good standing within the Catholic Church, returned with her family to Antwerp.

Cologne and Antwerp, where Peter Paul Rubens spent what seems to have been a happy childhood and adolescence, lay astride the uncertain frontier that divided Protestant from

Clara Serena Rubens

Nicolas Rubens

Rubens delighted in painting the members of his family. Above are two of his children, and opposite, the artist and his wife, Isabella, the very embodiment of a devoted young pair. Rubens was stricken with grief when Clara Serena died at the age of twelve; then he lost Isabella, in 1626, after seventeen years of marriage. Of her, he wrote: "She had no capricious moods, and no feminine weaknesses, but was all goodness and honesty." The Rubens home in Antwerp, with its ample studio, below, attracted patrons and distinguished visitors who, from the balcony, could watch the master working on as many as three canvases in one day, while assistants completed others in an upstairs room. Observing the prolific artist at work, one English visitor reported: "Usually Rubens would (with his Arms a cross) sit musing upon his work for some time, and in an instant in the liveliness of spirit, with a nimble hand, would force out his overcharged brain into description."

GUILLOT-TOP, PARIS

Rubens's studio, as restored some thirty years ago

Vincenzo Gonzaga

Archduchess Isabella

The patrons of Europe's most famous artist included several dukes and duchesses and more than a few kings and queens. Rubens started out as court painter to Vincenzo Gonzaga, the duke of Mantua, above left, whom he met while studying in Venice. In Spain, in 1603, he received his first important commission, an equestrian portrait of the duke of Lerma; he drew horse and rider, opposite, facing the viewer, a successful departure from the conventional pose in profile. As artist and roving diplomat, Rubens served the ruler of the Spanish Netherlands, Archduchess Isabella, above right, for nearly twenty-five years. In 1621, Marie de Médicis, the Queen Mother of France, hired him to do a series of twenty-one canvases (see pages 65 and 77 for two of them). His acquaintance with the handsome duke of Buckingham, below right, led to a major commission from England's Charles I. For his last royal patron, Philip IV of Spain, below left, he designed more than a hundred decorations for a hunting palace on the outskirts of Madrid.

Philip IV of Spain

The duke of Buckingham

Catholic Europe. As great trading cities, both were valuable prizes for the warring religious parties; both were hotly contested; and both were eventually brought back under Catholic control in the same year, 1585. The Rubens family left Cologne and settled in Antwerp at the very moment when the tide of the Counter Reformation was beginning to sweep back into both cities, bringing in its wake the emissaries of religious revival—the monks, the friars, and the priests whom the Protestants had rejected. Members of old religious orders that had been revitalized, like the Capuchins, and of new religious orders, like the Jesuits, set out to gain the young generation for the faith. Encouraged by their growing success, they founded schools and convents, built impressive new churches, and commissioned altarpieces and great decorative schemes that overwhelmed worshipers with a sense of the glory of God, the sufferings of the martyrs, and the victorious march of the Church Triumphant.

In this climate of an intense and revived Catholicism, Peter Paul Rubens grew up. It was a Catholicism that appealed directly and urgently to the senses, and its color and movement must have had a powerful attraction for anyone with as strong a visual sense as the young Rubens. "It is evident," he would one day write, "that religion exerts a stronger influence upon the human mind than any other motive." Throughout his life he remained a devoted Catholic, though his Catholicism was never narrow and exclusive. Like the rest of the intellectual aristocracy of Antwerp, Rubens was heir to the tolerant humanizing tradition of the Netherlands that is forever associated with Erasmus. He believed, as Erasmus had, that it was possible to harmonize the doctrines of Christianity and the wisdom of classical antiquity and to place the learning of ancient Greece and Rome at the service of the Church. To men who were secure in their faith, the pagan gods and goddesses, stripped of their power, were allegorical figures who could be set to work in a Christian environment, and pleasant traveling companions through the journey of life.

Erasmus had still dared to hope; but his late sixteenth-century successors, caught between the rival extremisms of Rome and Geneva, came close to despair. And in their despair they turned again to antiquity for consolation. They found it, of a sort, in the writings of Seneca. Stoicism, suitably tempered with Christianity, appeared to offer at least a partial answer to the troubles of the times. At any rate, this was the view of the leading Netherlands humanist of the age, Justus Lipsius, who took Rubens's brother Philip as a pupil. With Seneca, Lipsius counseled resignation: "We are obliged to endure novelties, and to refrain from troubling ourselves about what we cannot prevent." When Philip died suddenly in 1611, Peter Paul would commemorate his beloved brother in a group portrait showing him and Jan Woverius, a fellow scholar, seated at a table with the great Justus Lipsius, and, in a niche behind them, the bust of Seneca. It is no accident that the artist himself also appears in the picture, for he, too, imbibed, if only at second hand, the teachings of Lipsius and Seneca. It was perhaps from them that

Study for the equestrian portrait of the duke of Lerma, 1603

MUSEUM OF FINE ARTS, BOSTON

Studies of a river god, circa 1612–1615

The bearded figure above may well have been the model for the god of the Ganges, who strikes a similar pose in the gathering of continents and river gods, opposite. As Rubens imagined it, the meeting of Europe, Africa, America, and Asia, and their consorts, has the air of a family picnic; the adults relax while the babies romp with a friendly crocodile. Yet this fanciful allegory reveals Rubens's eye for realistic detail: he delights in arresting contrasts of texture, such as the play of infant flesh against scaly crocodile hide. Although the crocodile was probably based on a book illustration or an engraving, the tigress and her cubs, like the study of the lion below, may have been drawn from life, for he often sketched animals kept in menageries by his aristocratic friends.

BRITISH MUSEUM

A lion, circa 1614–1615

he learned to "free himself of every burden, like a swimmer in a stormy sea."

But if Rubens learned how to be detached, he could not be withdrawn or resigned to fate; his emotions were too strong, and his response to the human condition was too deep. When his first wife, Isabella Brandt, died in 1626, he would write to a friend about his grief: "I have no pretentions about ever attaining a stoic equanimity; I do not believe that human feelings so closely in accord with their object are unbecoming to man's nature, or that one can be equally indifferent to all things in this world. . . . Such a loss seems to me worthy of deep feeling."

The Stoicism that counseled the pursuit of equanimity taught, too, the need for constant self-discipline. This was another lesson that Rubens took to heart. When he was thirteen he spent a few months as a page in a noble household, acquiring there the polite manners and ease of bearing that later gained him approval at the courts of princes. But his urge to become an artist proved irresistible, and the page became an apprentice in a painter's studio. No apprentice was ever more conscientious and methodical. Though his extraordinary gifts were already evident, Rubens held them in check with a determined self-discipline, insisting on the acquisition of technique as his first priority.

It was possible to learn much about the craft of painting in the Netherlands, but the Netherlands, like all northern Europe, still looked to Italy as the fountainhead. In order to continue his education as an artist in the homeland of classical antiquity, which he already knew so well from his reading, Rubens left Antwerp in the spring of 1600 and set out for Italy. There he would spend the next eight years of his life, studying and copying classical models and the masterpieces of Renaissance and post-Renaissance art, displaying his virtuosity and establishing a European reputation.

The Italian years were critical for Rubens's artistic development. He immersed himself in the classical culture that was to afford him such pleasure and inspiration throughout his working life, and he absorbed the full impact of Italian Counter Reformation art, triumphantly displayed in the Rome of the great Sixtus V and his successors. There, in the basilica of St. Peter's, in the splendid Jesuit church of the Gesù, in the palaces of cardinals, and in numerous churches and convents, he saw and admired the work of the new generation of Italian artists and craftsmen. His contemporaries, Annibale Carracci, Domenichino, Guido Reni, the reckless Caravaggio, all were grappling with the problem that preoccupied Rubens—how to escape the clichés of the Mannerist style and represent traditional themes and the familiar dramas of the Old and New Testaments with a new spontaneity. Rubens's solution, which came only after years of trial and effort, exactly reflected his genius and his temperament. In his great religious paintings, the *Adoration of the Kings* of 1609–10, for instance, and the *Descent from the Cross* of 1611–14, pathos is expressed in sweeping curves and richly orchestrated colors. But the drama is under control, and it is that extraordinary confrontation of energy and discipline that

THE FOUR QUARTERS OF THE GLOBE, circa 1615–1616

gives Rubens's religious works their inner dynamic and stamped them so forcefully on the consciousness of his age.

Rubens, however, was too versatile, too interested in everything, to let himself be typecast as a religious artist. Titian, whom he greatly admired, had excelled both in portraiture and in representations of classical mythology. Rubens would do no less. Artists in the seventeenth century, however, were not their own masters. Though the achievements of some of their recent predecessors had done something to enhance their social status, they remained essentially craftsmen, practitioners of the mechanical arts, dependent on the commissions of patrons, enlightened or unenlightened.

Given the circumstances of his time, Rubens was fortunate in his first major patron, Duke Vincenzo of Mantua. Though the duke had little to recommend him personally, he enthusiastically continued the Gonzaga family tradition of lavish artistic patronage. Discovering the work of Rubens on a visit to Venice in 1600, he offered the artist a place in his service. It was, therefore, under the duke of Mantua's auspices that Rubens lived and worked in Italy. His position often involved him in tedious commissions for his ducal master, but it also provided him with financial security, valuable social connections, and, above all, the opportunity to study. Mantua in the early seventeenth century was an artistic treasure house. In the Palazzo del Tè, the summer palace designed and decorated by Giulio Romano, Rubens could contemplate the overwhelming frescoes of *The Fall of the Titans*. In the ducal galleries he could spend hours before the Mantegnas, the Raphaels, the Titians, the Tintorettos, the Correggios, and the Veroneses.

His time in Italy was not, however, spent entirely in Mantua, for the duke, a restless voluptuary and congenital traveler, was happy to let Rubens travel. He went not only to the major cities of Italy but also, in 1603, to Spain. The duke had commissioned him to deliver a series of conciliatory gifts to Philip III—rock-crystal vases, a coach with six bay horses, and for the duke of Lerma, the king's favorite and a man with a taste for the arts,

KUNSTHISTORISCHES MUSEUM, VIENNA

THE LITTLE FUR, circa 1638

Her fair skin glowing against a dark fur cloak, Helena Fourment, Rubens's second wife, exhibits the beauty—and sheer avoirdupois—that the aging artist unabashedly adored. Helena was only sixteen and he was fifty-three when they married in 1630, and the match scandalized Antwerp society. But, by all accounts, they were extraordinarily happy. Certainly Rubens was infatuated, and Helena's face and figure appear repeatedly in his later work. During the last five years of his life, Rubens had a country retreat at Steen, and there, perhaps, he painted Helena seated with two of their five children, opposite.

copies of sixteen pictures in the Mantuan collection. Unfortunately Lerma's pictures were damaged in transit, and Rubens had a hectic time surreptitiously restoring them before finally handing them over at the court in Valladolid.

The visit to Spain gave Rubens a chance to see the superb royal collection of Titians in the Escorial, and it also gave him his first introduction to the world of high politics and diplomacy. In particular, he attracted the attention of the duke of Lerma, of whom he painted an unusual equestrian portrait (see page 69). For a man who would later represent his government in delicate diplomatic negotiations, such contacts in Spain would prove highly advantageous. Shortly before his death Philip II had nominally made over the loyal provinces of the Netherlands to his daughter Isabella and her husband, the Hapsburg Archduke Albert, but they still belonged inexorably to the Hispanic world and would continue to do so as long as they were dependent on Spanish aid in their struggle against the rebellious Protestant provinces to the north. Ties between the Spanish court and Brussels, capital of the southern provinces, were close, if not cordial, and Rubens, as a loyalist Netherlander, was to find easy acceptance in that community of peoples and provinces that owed allegiance to the king of Spain.

He felt more at home, however, in a wider international community—that of arts and letters. The *lingua franca* was still Latin, although Italian was now beginning to replace it, and Rubens wrote his letters in Italian, not Spanish, occasionally resorting to French or his native Flemish. Yet for all his newfound cosmopolitanism, he reserved his deepest loyalties for his northern homeland. A visit to Genoa in 1607 must have acted as a powerful reminder of his native Antwerp, for Genoa was to the Mediterranean world what Antwerp, before the wars, had been to northern Europe—a center of international trade and finance, and a prosperous port city governed by a wealthy urban aristocracy. Rubens painted the portraits of some of these Genoese patricians, and he closely studied the design of the spacious town houses where they lived their comfortable lives. These houses suggested to him a pattern of living that he felt was immediately applicable to Antwerp. When he eventually returned home in 1608 and bought himself a house, he would proceed to remodel it in the Italian manner, and in Antwerp in 1622 he would publish a volume of plans and engravings of the palaces of Genoa.

It would require more than house plans, however, to transform the ailing Antwerp of the early seventeenth century into a Genoa of the north. The rival city of Amsterdam, in the northern Netherlands, had siphoned off much of its trade; the growing economic power of the Protestant United Provinces had sapped the vitality of the loyalist south. Under the benign and concerned government of the "archdukes," Albert and Isabella, the south was gradually beginning to recover confidence, but as long as Spain continued to war with the rebellious provinces in the north, the process would be slow. In 1609, however, mutual exhaustion brought, if not permanent peace, at least a twelve-year truce. While the terms of the truce were unfavorable to the economic recovery of Antwerp, peace itself provided a breathing space for the hard-pressed southern provinces. Slowly, coaxed along by Archduke Albert and, after his death in 1621, by the benevolent care of Archduchess Isabella, the southern provinces began to coalesce into a society with an identity profoundly different from that of the nascent Dutch Republic to the north. The northern provinces were becoming a brash, dynamic Protestant society dominated by a mercantile oligarchy, which considered liberty and a fair degree of religious tolerance as the essential ingredients of commercial success. The Spanish Netherlands of the south, by contrast, clung fast to the traditional values. They were monarchical rather than republican, aristocratic rather than bourgeois, and profoundly Catholic.

If economic growth is the measure of a successful society, the Dutch Republic wins hands down. But if it is the arts of civilization, the scales are more evenly balanced. The brilliant cultural successes of the Dutch Republic—the society that produced Hals, Rembrandt, Vermeer—have tended to overshadow the remarkable achievements of the south. If any single figure can be held responsible for developing the richly textured civilization of the Spanish Netherlands, it was Peter Paul Rubens.

In 1608 Rubens, learning that his mother was dying, hurried home from Italy. He may have intended to return to Italy, but his reputation had preceded him to the Netherlands, and Albert and Isabella were quick to offer him the post of court painter. The offer encouraged him to establish himself in Antwerp. Here in 1609 he married Isabella Brandt, the daughter of a lawyer, and after the birth of their first child they settled down in a large house to which Rubens added a spacious studio. Years of extraordinary productivity followed. There were commissions from the court; commissions from churches and religious orders (the Jesuits, for example, requested a vast decorative scheme for their church of St. Charles Borromeo in Antwerp); and an ever-lengthening list of commissions from an international clientele. Indeed, the fame of his creative genius

LOUVRE — GIRAUDON

HELENA FOURMENT AND HER CHILDREN, circa 1636

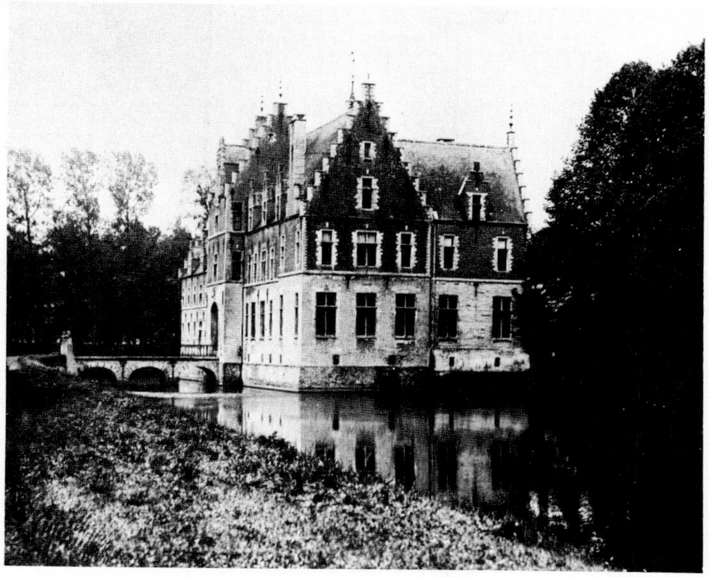
ROGER-VIOLLET, PARIS

The Rubens château at Steen

rapidly transformed Antwerp into Europe's new artistic center. Promising young artists—Anthony van Dyck among them—competed to secure entry to his studio, foreign connoisseurs came reverently to watch the great man at work, and the princes and aristocracy of Europe bargained for his masterpieces.

Nor, on the whole, were his patrons disappointed. His prices were stiff but fair, and what he promised he delivered. Above all, he was prepared to tackle anything, and the larger and more daunting the project, the better. So it was that, in the early 1620's, he threw himself into the great scheme devised by Marie de Médicis, the queen mother of France, for a monumental pictorial cycle that would hang in the Luxembourg Palace in Paris and commemorate the events of her career and that of the late king, Henry IV. Since her life history had hardly been glorious, the project required both tact and imagination, but Rubens rose triumphantly to the occasion. His twenty-one vast canvases magnificently celebrate, in a form more allegorical than historical, the triumphs and vicissitudes of Marie de Médicis's tempestuous life. To his regret, the commission for the other cycle, representing the career of Henry IV, fell through.

A Danish visitor to the Antwerp studio just before Rubens embarked on the Marie de Médicis cycle gives us a vivid picture of the artist at work. "Though occupied with his painting, he was listening to a reading from Tacitus and, at the same time, dictating a letter. We kept silent for fear of disturbing him, but he addressed us without interrupting his work; all the while having the reading continued and still dictating the letter, he answered our questions as though to give us proof of his powerful faculties." No doubt Rubens was assiduously cultivating his public *persona* for the occasion, yet this vignette of the artist in his studio reveals why his output was so prodigious. Under the pressure of numerous commissions, he came to make heavy use of his studio assistants; yet the inspiring genius and the controlling mind remained his. Exceptional stamina and vitality, allied with an enormous capacity for concentration and for organizing, enabled him to make the most of his crowded working day. He was interested in everything; he appears to have enjoyed everything; and in his voluminous correspondence with a network of humanist friends, he moves easily from discussion of public events to the details of his latest commission and on to a learned discourse of some recently discovered Roman cameo, commenting on each subject in turn with shrewdness, elegance, and a remarkable generosity of spirit.

Behind this extraordinarily versatile performance lay a profound domestic stability. It was tragically interrupted by the death of Isabella in 1626 but renewed in the last decade of his life by his marriage to the entrancing Helena Fourment, who was to bear him five children in ten years. The combination of domestic felicity and international lionizing could easily have gone to the head of a lesser man, but Rubens, while always conscious of his own worth, somehow preserved his modesty and his sense of proportion.

The truce between Spain and the United Provinces expired in 1621. War returned to the Spanish Netherlands, and, as the years passed, merged into that wider conflict between Protestants and Catholics, the Thirty Years' War. The misery and devastation of war were a source of anguish to Rubens, who was, in his own words, "by nature and inclination a peaceful man." "For my own part," he wrote in 1627, "I should like the whole world to be in peace, that we might live in a golden age instead of an age of iron."

But as the reluctant dweller in an age of iron, Rubens could not evade the rigors it inevitably imposed. During the 1620's Archduchess Isabella, together with Ambrogio di Spinola, the Genoese commander in chief of the Spanish army of the Netherlands, did everything possible to extricate the southern provinces from a war that threatened to engulf them in ruin. Tied to Madrid, which was heavily committed to the international conflict, the government in Brussels had little opportunity for independent maneuvering. But it could indulge in a little diplomatic probing on its own, hoping desperately that some rapprochement between Spain and England might bring peace closer. For this delicate diplomatic work, the archduchess needed a confidential agent whom she fully trusted and whose movements would not arouse suspicion. What better choice than Rubens, who had an entrée to all the courts of

BOTH: ALTE PINAKOTHEK, MUNICH

THE RAPE OF THE DAUGHTERS OF LEUCIPPUS, 1615–1617. Right: detail

The abduction of two mortal women by the demigods Castor and Pollux is a swirling Baroque composition as well as a bountiful display of female flesh. The massive nudes, their every curve and dimple clearly delineated, reflect light as if their skin were heavy satin.

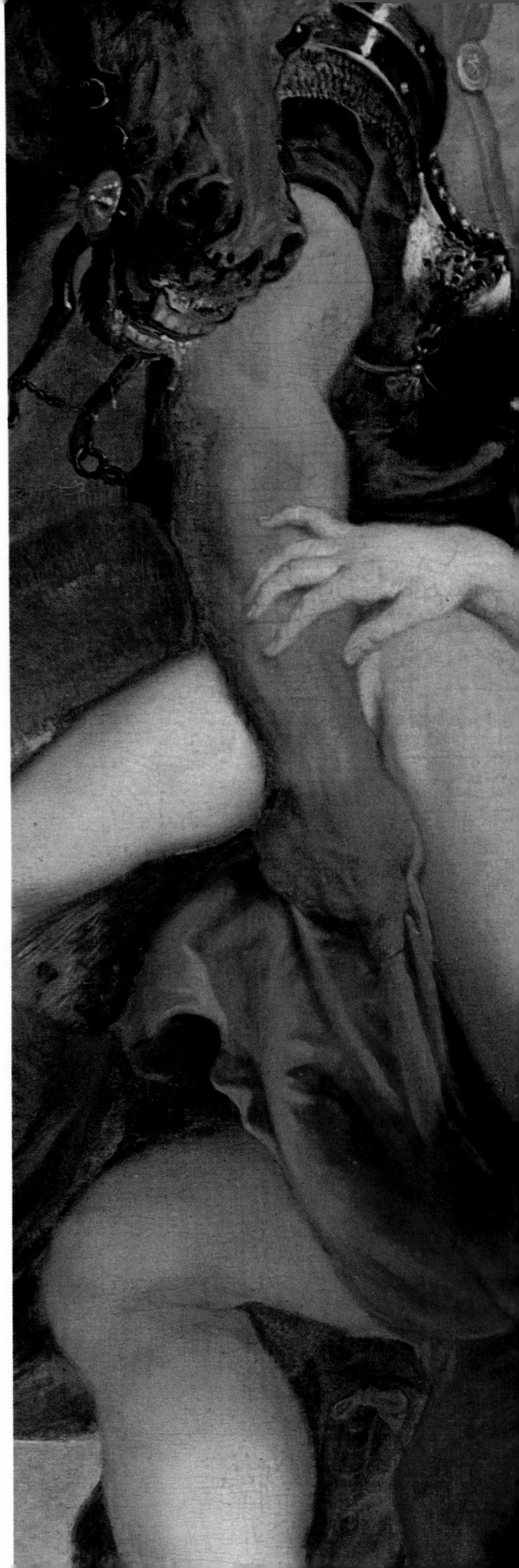

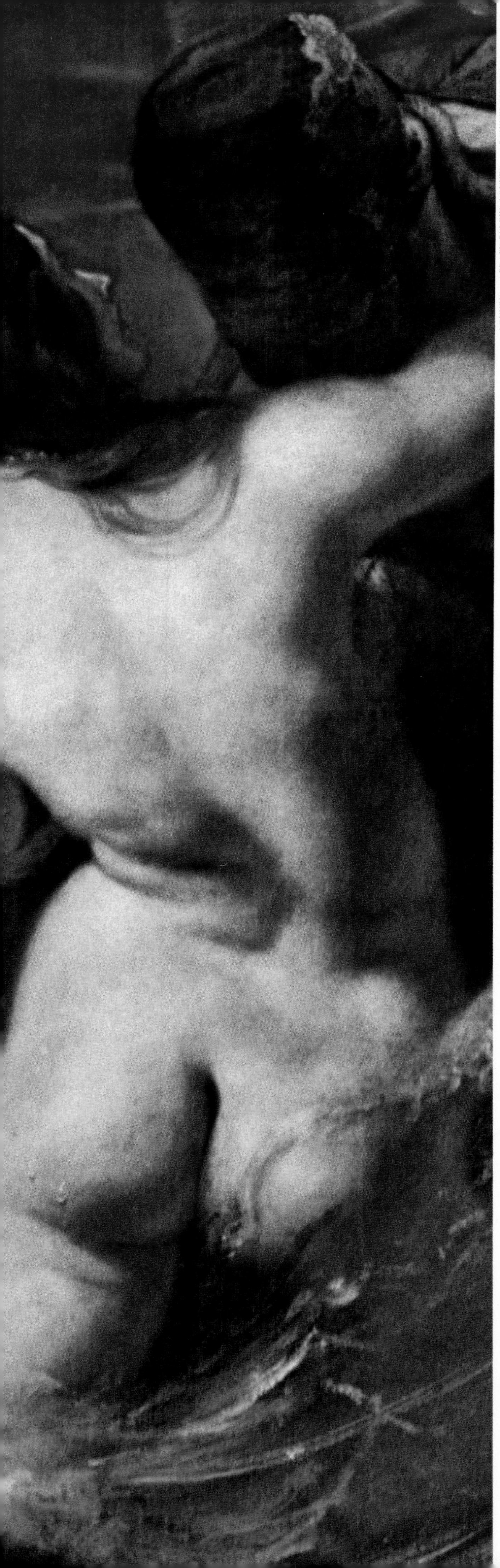

Europe, and who could pursue a quiet diplomacy under the convenient cover of his legitimate artistic activities?

So it was that Rubens started on his travels again. In Paris in 1625, he had met that great patron the duke of Buckingham, the favorite of Charles I of England; in 1626 he had successfully negotiated with Balthasar Gerbier, Buckingham's agent, for the duke's purchase of his collection of Roman antiquities. And now, in 1627, on a tour of Holland he combined art with diplomacy, meeting with Gerbier and the English ambassador to The Hague. Soon afterward he was summoned to Spain to report on his activities.

Twenty-five years had passed since his last visit to Spain, and in the intervening period much had changed. The bland duke of Lerma, the favorite of Philip III, had been replaced by the dynamic and aggressive Olivares, the favorite of the new king, Philip IV. Rubens's long conversations with Olivares still left him time to paint the king and the royal family and form a close friendship with the promising new court painter, Diego Velázquez. It was not the least of Rubens's achievements that he was able to introduce Velázquez, at a critical moment in his career, to the latest developments in European painting.

After eight months in Spain he returned to Brussels by way of France, allowing himself just enough time to have a look at his Marie de Médicis cycle, now magnificently installed in the Luxembourg Palace. Then, in 1629, he was off again on another diplomatic mission, this time across the Channel to the court of Charles I. England came as a surprise to him. For a country so remote from Italy it proved remarkably civilized, and Rubens found himself in a court presided over by a monarch of exquisite aesthetic sensibilities. Rubens, with his tact, his refinement, and his deep knowledge of the arts, cut an appealing figure. Before he left he collected a Cambridge doctorate, a knighthood, and a challenging artistic commission—the decoration of the ceiling of Inigo Jones's magnificent Banqueting

THE ARRIVAL OF MARIE DE MÉDICIS AT MARSEILLES, 1623–1625. Left: detail

Married by proxy, Marie de Médicis, having sailed to France to meet her bridegroom, Henry IV, encounters a joyful committee of gods, goddesses, and sea creatures who welcome her to port at Marseilles. The mermaids, their abundant forms twisting and turning with superhuman energy, virtually soar out of the sea toward the future queen.

House in Whitehall with a series of paintings on a theme hardly less equivocal than that of the life of Marie de Médicis: the blessings of the reign of the late James I.

The Anglo-Spanish peace of 1630 was a tribute to the tact and discretion with which Rubens had performed his missions, but it also marked the culmination (and virtual conclusion) of his diplomatic career. In 1633 Archduchess Isabella died, and her successor, the Cardinal Infant Don Fernando, the brother of Philip IV, had less need of his services. Rubens himself had acquired, as he wrote in 1636, "a horror of courts," and as he grew older he turned increasingly to the simpler pleasures of the countryside and of family life. He had bought himself a country manor house, the Château de Steen, as a place of retreat from Antwerp; and here, in his relative retirement, he devoted many hours to exploring and painting the beauties of the Flemish landscape. Although his right hand became arthritic, his versatility and creativity remained with him to the end.

Rubens died in Antwerp on May 30, 1640, at peace with himself and with the world. For a generation he had dominated Europe's artistic life, and he had done so with a generosity and largeness of mind that made envy difficult. In his work, as in his personality, he unerringly recognized the point of equilibrium between opposing extremes. Here was a Christian who responded wholeheartedly to the classical culture of pagan antiquity; a Catholic who was acceptable to Protestants; a bourgeois who, in the words of his epitaph, "made himself a pathway of friendship to kings and princes"; a Northern European who understood and assimilated the civilization of the Mediterranean lands. His overflowing vitality was matched by an equally remarkable serenity of mind. Forever dynamic and yet in full command, Rubens miraculously reconciled in his life and in his art the restless energy and the controlled power that constituted the reality and the aspirations of the age of the Baroque.

J. H. Elliott, professor of history at Princeton's Institute for Advanced Study, wrote on Mannerism in HORIZON, *Summer, 1973.*

BOTH: KUNSTHISTORISCHES MUSEUM, VIENNA

THE FEAST OF VENUS, circa 1630–1640. Right: detail

Bouncing cupids are everywhere, even in the trees, in this orgiastic celebration of love, perhaps inspired by Helena Fourment (who was, in fact, the model for the nymph at far left, above.) Their arms intertwined, the nymphs and satyrs at right dance across a garden of love in a feverish pas de quatre, *exuding a warmth and softness that are nearly palpable.*

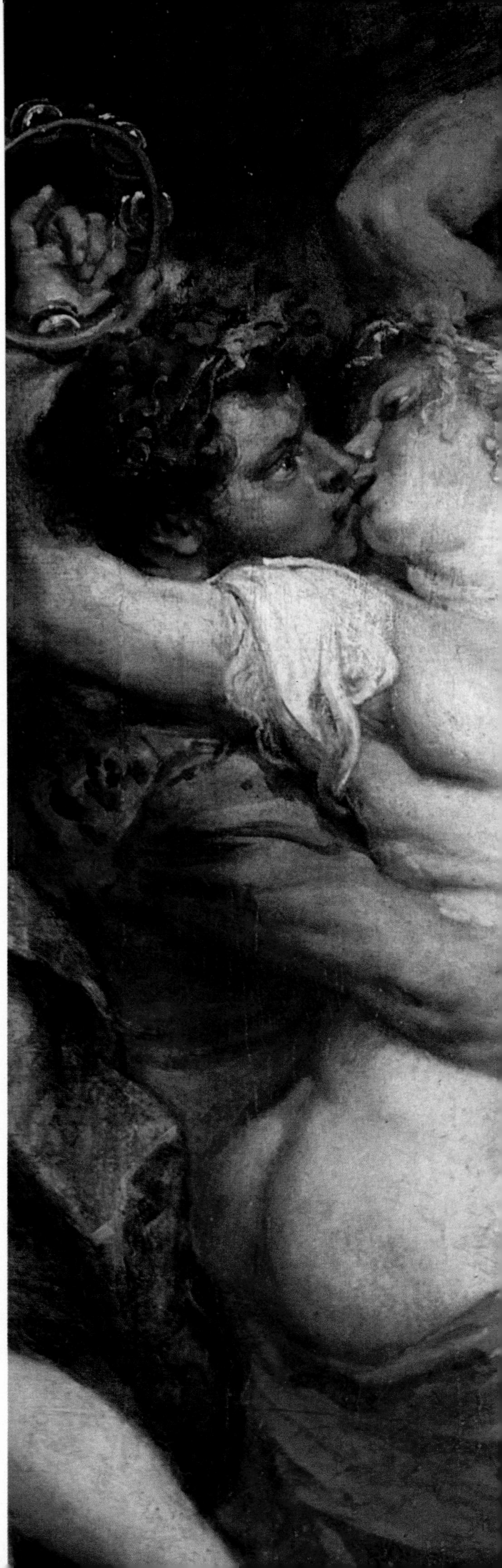

A Life in the Theatre

How a great actor and director gave Shakespeare to the twentieth century

In 1970 the Royal Shakespeare Company came to New York with Peter Brook's production of *A Midsummer Night's Dream*, which was hailed as revolutionary. In some ways that was true, but what was generally unknown was that Brook's production was in a revolutionary tradition, a tradition begun before World War I by the English director Harley Granville Barker. "Barker's productions at the Savoy from 1912 to 1914," Robert Speaight has written in *Shakespeare on the Stage*, "looked ahead in a pretty straight line to Peter Brook's *A Midsummer Night's Dream* at Stratford more than fifty years later." For it was Barker who pioneered in stripping Shakespearean production of nineteenth-century scenic and musical baggage.

FROM PURDOM, *Harley Granville Barker*, BARIE AND ROCKLIFFE, LONDON, 1956

Harley Granville Barker studies Shakespeare's First Folio in Glasgow in 1910. Seventeen years later he began publishing his Prefaces to Shakespeare, *masterful critiques of fourteen of the plays.*

My point is not to diminish Brook, who has inherited from the past as all alert artists must, but to identify and explore that inheritance. Granville Barker is one of the most extraordinary and extraordinarily versatile figures in the history of the English-speaking theatre, an artist whose influence, long after his death, remains strong on both sides of the Atlantic even when his name is unknown. (The very spelling of that name is a bit of a muddle. After his second marriage Barker hyphenated his middle and last names, so some indexes list him as Granville-Barker, Harley. His biographer, C. B. Purdom, calls him Barker, and I'll follow suit.)

Early in his life Barker reportedly said that he planned to spend ten years as an actor, ten as a director, and the rest of his life as a writer. He did hold more or less to that schedule, though the decades overlapped somewhat. Presumably he meant that in his later years he would concentrate on playwriting, which he had begun early, and he did indeed write some plays and translate many in those years; but what he did not foresee was that he would spend his last twenty-five years out of the working theatre—as a scholar, principally concerned with the essays by which he is now best known, his *Prefaces to Shakespeare.*

All four of those careers had their true distinctions. His acting made a strong impression on many critics. Max Beerbohm wrote of one Barker performance in 1904 that it had "just that mastery of climax and anti-climax which makes an artistic whole." Of his directing, John Gielgud, who worked with Barker in 1940 on one of his rare returns to the theatre, said: "I never saw actors watch a director with such utter admiration and obedience. It was like Toscanini coming to a rehearsal." Of his playwriting, J. B. Priestley said in 1967 that Barker "is undoubtedly one of the most original, intelligent, and sensitive English dramatists of this century." And of his *Prefaces* Arthur M. Eastman says in *A Short History of Shakespearean Criticism*, published in 1968, that Barker, as no one else in that history, "helps us to a sense of the stage actuality of a Shakespearean play."

It is possible—possibly easy—to fault Baker in each of his four pro-

By STANLEY KAUFFMANN

fessions, but the fact that he achieved genuine eminence in all four of them stamps him a genius. What makes him relevant today, not just a rueful-fascinating historical figure, is the way he affected the theatre in which some of us work and which all of us attend. What makes him biographically interesting are the elements of tragedy in his life, tragedy that is endemic to the theatre.

Barker was born in London in 1877, the son of a rather nebulous real-estate agent who was descended from clergymen. His mother, much more influential on him, was the granddaughter of an Italian physician who had emigrated to England. (Bernard Shaw, who met Barker at the turn of the century, said that the younger man "had a strong strain of Italian blood in him and looked as if he had stepped out of a picture by Benozzo Gozzoli.") Mrs. Barker was the chief breadwinner of the family by means of a then popular entertainment, the poetry recital. She toured Britain and America. Her son could not have had much formal education—the first anomaly in a career marked by intellectual rigor—because he spent much of his childhood traveling with her and at times recited items on the program.

He made his first appearance as actor in a provincial English theatre in 1891, and the following year, aged fifteen, made his London debut as a "3rd Young Man." Evidently he showed some quality, although he was no immediate sensation, because he kept finding work and kept progressing.

About this time Barker began writing plays. His first, a collaboration called *The Weather-hen*, was produced in London with some success in 1899. Barker was twenty-two. That year he read a minor role in a copyrighting performance of Shaw's new play *Caesar and Cleopatra*. In those days the copyright law was such that at least one public performance of a play had to be given in order for the author to hold his rights. (Sometimes he would merely get some friends, actors or otherwise, to come to a hall one morning, tack a hastily scrawled performance notice on the board outside, and have his friends read the script aloud on stage.) The importance of this particular performance was, first, that Barker was selected for it, and, second, that it brought him together with the forty-three-year-old Shaw and thus helped initiate a great era in the English theatre.

The meeting of Barker and Shaw helped change the latter from a published but rarely performed dramatist into a famous theatre artist in Britain and, soon, the world. Barker did this partly by his acting of important Shaw roles. Shaw said he was "humanly speaking, perfect" as Marchbanks in *Candida*, which he played in 1900, and subsequently Barker played in the first productions of *Man and Superman* (John Tanner), *John Bull's Other Island* (Father Keegan), *Major Barbara* (Adolphus Cusins), and *The Doctor's Dilemma* (Louis Dubedat). He influenced Shaw because, quite inferably, the author had him in mind when writing those roles and because his performances contributed substantially to the productions that ensured Shaw's theatrical place. That might have been monument enough, to have been inspiration and executant for a great dramatist, but it was a lesser part of Barker's career, even of his contribution to Shaw's career.

Barker had begun directing in 1900, and by 1904, at the age of twenty-seven, he had done five productions, including a bill of short plays, two of them by Maeterlinck, and a full-length play of his own, *The Marrying of Ann Leete*. Then came two significant events. He married Lillah McCarthy, a stunning, exceptionally gifted actress with whom he had once toured; and he joined forces with a manager named J. E. Vedrenne to run the Royal Court Theatre (nowadays known as the home of the English Stage Company, producers of John Osborne and other prominent playwrights of the last twenty years).

The Barker-Vedrenne partnership was no ordinary managerial move. It was, as it turned out, the major effort of Barker's life toward the goal that mattered most in his life: the establishment of a permanent theatre of high quality. He and the critic William Archer had already written a book-length study called *Scheme and Estimates for a National Theatre* that set forth, in ostensibly practical terms, the means to realize a vision. The means was not forthcoming, so Barker sought another avenue. He and Vedrenne decided to do a series of matinees of plays of merit. They began in October, 1904, with some backing from friends, including Shaw, and by the following February they took over the theatre completely.

The Barker-Vedrenne management of the Royal Court lasted until June, 1907, when money difficulties intervened, but during that relatively brief time it changed the shape and intent, even the frustrations, of the English theatre. From that time on, the level of playwriting, of general artistic tenor, was affected by the Royal Court venture: achievement and disappointment in the theatre were measured against the Barker-Vedrenne record.

In the course of those three years the Barker-Vedrenne management gave 988 performances. Shaw loomed largest in the list with 701 performances of 11 of his plays. They also produced plays by Euripides (in Gilbert Murray's new translations), Ibsen, Galsworthy, Hauptmann, Schnitzler, Yeats, Mase-

Those Slapdash Elizabethans

Shakespeare was working in the youth of an art, to which . . . freedom is more allowable. Let us not suppose, though, that, for all their seemingly slapdash ways, these Elizabethan dramatists would not be concerned with the technique of their craft. . . . They did not write books, or have to listen to lectures on the subject. . . . But . . . the little group of comrades and rivals would bandy sharp personal criticism upon work in the doing with the religious fervor which properly belongs to a living art.

—Harley Granville Barker, "From *Henry V* to *Hamlet*," in *More Prefaces to Shakespeare*, Princeton University Press, 1974.

field, and Barker himself. He directed many of the plays and acted in many, sometimes in those he also directed.

Seasons of serious new plays are not unfamiliar phenomena these days (partly because of Barker's effect, here as in Britain), but in those days such seasons were virtually unknown. The previous century had been one pre-eminently of acting, usually star-centered rather than ensemble work, and of generally abysmal playwriting, usually tailor-made for stars. The intellectual and aesthetic changes that were already roaring through the other arts and that had already blown away much of the fustiness in continental playwriting had left the English-language theatre almost untouched. This director-actor-playwright, twenty-seven when he joined with Vedrenne, changed all that in just three years. He did not move our theatre en bloc to Parnassus, but from then on it could at least know what it was missing. Further, perhaps foremost, it established Shaw in the position from which he has not yet been budged: as the greatest dramatist after Shakespeare in our language.

It also established Barker. At thirty he was now a figure of first consequence. The end of the Royal Court days marked the end of the ten years as actor that he had "scheduled" for himself; he acted very little thereafter. Now he concentrated on directing, which profited enormously from his acting talent and experience, and on writing plays. His first play of lasting worth, *The Voysey Inheritance*, had been produced at the Royal Court in 1905, directed by himself with himself in the leading role. The plot concerns a respected old solicitor who, just before he dies, informs his son and partner that the firm is operating fraudulently. The son must decide whether to expose matters and bring about ruin or keep up the fraud until he can set things right.

In 1907 came *Waste*, again directed by Barker with himself in the leading role, a play about a brilliant young politician who has a casual affair that wrecks his career and prevents him from

BOTH: RAYMOND MANDER AND JOE MITCHENSON THEATRE COLLECTION

Lillah McCarthy in 1910

Barker married Lillah McCarthy in 1906, and they appeared together, on stage and off, until 1915. In that year Barker met Helen Huntington, a wealthy woman some twelve years his senior. Their marriage, in 1918, precipitated the break between Barker and Shaw.

Helen Huntington, circa 1895

doing the great good he might have done his country. In 1909 came *The Madras House*, directed by Barker but without him in the cast. *The Madras House*, too, deals with inheritance of a sort—the passing of a successful fashion house from father to son—but thematically it deals with changes in men's view of women and with women's changing view of themselves.

All three of these plays contain elements of, in Max Beerbohm's phrase, "breadth and brilliancy." All three of them show, again in Beerbohm's phrase, how "deeply influenced he was and is" by Shaw. Still, of all the dramatists influenced by Shaw, Barker is easily the best, and if his "original contributions to our dramatic literature" are not quite the "treasures" that Shaw called them in his obituary article, they are still far too good for oblivion.

Paradoxically, his plays, his works in permanently available form, have had less effect on the theatre than his work in ephemeral form: his directing. His production of new plays at the Royal Court and elsewhere had demonstrated his diamond-bright intelligence, his hatred of stagy cliché, his great sensitivity to character nuance, his extraordinary ear. Now he began to apply these attributes to Shakespeare. To some his work seemed raw and disturbing, but his intent was to unite the best of what he took to be the Elizabethan manner with the best of the modern. He believed in suppleness of verse-speaking (music but not music for its own sake) and the speed of speech and action that are implicit in the very structure of the Elizabethan stage; he believed in simple design and costume and lighting—chaste and strong, rather than lots of stage freight and upholstery.

With the aid of a rich peer, Barker was able to make one more attempt at establishing the beginnings of a theatre close to his ideal, at the Savoy. He was highly dissatisfied with the job-lot life of the commercial theatre, so much so that he had even talked about emigrating to Germany and becoming a naturalized citizen there. Several visits to that country had strongly impressed him with German regard for the institution of the theatre and willingness to subsidize it (which is still true). But at least he was able to start work at the Savoy.

His productions of Shakespeare there began with *The Winter's Tale* in September, 1912. Critics said it was not Shakespeare, it was postimpressionism. Amid the uproar, writes C. B. Purdom, "there were those who recognized new factors . . . freedom from subservience to the actor-manager, freedom from elaborate staging, faithfulness to the text, and the conviction that Shakespeare was not a dead classic but a dramatist for the twentieth-century theatre."

Two months later Barker produced *Twelfth Night* at the Savoy. Other work intervened, and he did his last Shakespeare production, *A Midsummer Night's Dream*, at the Savoy in February, 1914. In his entire career he directed only four Shakespeare plays—there had been a production of *Two Gentlemen of Verona* ten years earlier—but they have touched the theatre's thinking about Shakespeare ever since.

His ten years as playwright were overlapped by his ten as director. And those years in turn were overlapped, were ended at last in a way that wrenched him out of his whole style of life.

In the winter of 1915 Barker brought three productions to New York: Shaw's *Androcles and the Lion*, Anatole France's *The Man Who Married a Dumb Wife*, and Shakespeare's *Midsummer Night's Dream*. Press and public were startled but engaged, as they were by the two productions of Greek plays that Barker did in American college stadiums in the summer of 1915. Then a change, sudden and profound, came in Barker's private life.

In a sense not at all cynical, this change might be said to reflect a desire, perhaps unconscious, to emulate Shaw even further. Barker's playwriting, as noted, was indebted to Shaw. He joined the socialist Fabian Society, in which Shaw was prominent, and he resigned from the executive board of that society when Shaw did (although Shaw remained a socialist all his life while Barker filtered away). The very example of professional versatility, though Barker's was much lesser, was set by Shaw. Now a different sort of example may possibly have affected Barker: Shaw's marriage to an adoring rich woman.

Barker's own marriage to Lillah McCarthy had seemingly been good. They had worked together at the Royal Court and the Savoy, and she was with him in America playing leading roles for him. But in New York Barker met Helen Huntington, the wife of an American multimillionaire, and they fell in love. His affection for her was genuine: there is no more reason to doubt that in his case than in Shaw's. (More reason to believe it in Barker's case, perhaps, because, unlike Charlotte Shaw, Mrs. Huntington was not rich in her own right. Her husband had endowed her generously when they parted.) But given the importance of Shaw in Barker's life, it is hard to believe that some idea of living à la Shaw did not occur to Barker.

The effect on Lillah was cruel, devastating. She left America with Barker in June, 1915, believing that his relationship with Helen was over. But he was back in New York in September without her, and in January of 1916 Lillah got a letter from him asking for a divorce. "She went at once to Shaw," says Purdom, "who said that he, too, had heard from Barker by the same post." Years later Lillah described that evening in a passage from her memoirs that was omitted from the published book (all references to Barker were deleted, at his insistence):

> I went all frozen on a cold January night. . . . Shaw greeted me very tenderly and made me sit by the fire. I was shivering. Shaw sat very still. . . . How long we sat there I do not know, but presently I found myself walking with dragging steps with Shaw beside me . . . up and down Adelphi Terrace. . . . He let me cry. Presently I heard a voice in which all the gentleness and tenderness of the world was speaking. It said: "Look up, dear, look up to the heavens. There is more in life than this. There is much more."

If that sounds unlike the usual image of Shaw, it fits the image of a protective parent, which is how he saw himself in relation to the young genius and his gifted, beautiful wife. After Barker returned to England, Shaw saw him as often as he could, despite his sympathy for Lillah, but the friendship could not continue. Barker's new wife detested both Shaw and the theatre itself. She felt that the workaday theatre was an unworthy place for a man of Barker's intellect and writing abilities, and she disliked Shaw, possibly because he was a link with and reminder of Lillah, but more surely because he was happy in the theatre, appreciated Barker's gigantic theatrical gifts, and wanted him to keep on using them.

Unquestionably Shaw was grievously hurt by the breach, though he sometimes spoke lightly of it. He wasn't even informed of the second marriage, which took place in July, 1918. A month later Shaw wrote to Barker: "It would be convenient occasionally to know something about you. I surmise that you are married; but it is only a surmise. . . . I have refrained, with an exaggerated delicacy, from asking you questions for a year or so. Now I do ask them bluntly." The reply is not known, although they met later that year.

Unquestionably Shaw had looked on

To Gabble or Not to Gabble

I think that all Elizabethan dramatic verse must be spoken swiftly, and nothing can make me think otherwise. My fellow workers acting in *The Winter's Tale* were accused by some people (only by some) of gabbling. I readily take that accusation on myself, and I deny it. Gabbling implies hasty speech, but our ideal was speed, nor was the speed universal, nor, but in a dozen well-defined passages, really so great. Unexpected it was, I don't doubt; and once exceed the legal limit, as well accuse you of seventy miles an hour as twenty-one. But I call in question the evidence of mere policemen-critics. I question a little their expertness of hearing, a little too their quickness of understanding Elizabethan English not at its easiest, just a little their lack of delight in anything that is not as they thought it always would be, and I suggest that it is more difficult than they think to look and listen and remember and appraise all in the same flash of time. But be all the shortcomings on one side, and that side ours, it is still no proof that the thing come short of is not the right thing. That is the important point to determine. . . .

—Harley Granville Barker, "*Twelfth Night*," in *More Prefaces to Shakespeare*, Princeton, 1974.

Barker as a son-in-art. (At one time there was even a rumor in London that Barker was his natural son.) In his biography of Shaw, the Irish critic-playwright St. John Ervine says that a few years after the second marriage, he was driving in the country with Shaw and they passed the road that led up to Barker's palatial new home. "I said to G.B.S.: 'Harley Granville-Barker lives up that road.' He looked at it in the odd way he had when he was moved, and, almost as if he were indifferent, said, 'Oh, Harley!' But when G.B.S. was as terse as that he was under deep emotion."

Thus, if Barker had made his second marriage because he was consciously or unconsciously modeling himself on Shaw, the result was to split him from his model. It was a Shavian irony.

His marriage was also to split him from the theatre. After 1918 until his death in 1946, save for a few excursions, most of them quite brief, he did nothing in the theatre. He wrote about the theatre, principally a book called *The Exemplary Theatre* in which he restated his aims for the theatre he had not been able to make and argued for a closer relationship between the university and the theatre. He lectured from time to time. He translated, some French plays on his own, some Spanish ones with his wife. He finished his fourteen illuminating *Prefaces to Shakespeare*, each one an essay on a particular play, the one on *Hamlet* so long that it is a complete book in itself.

And he wrote two more plays, of debatable quality but of high vicarious interest. *The Secret Life* (1923) is about a retired English politician who is persuaded to run again for Parliament and a probable cabinet post, but who quits the campaign to visit the woman he loves, who is dying—in America! *His Majesty* (1928) is about an exiled king who makes an effort to regain his crown but is sent again into exile. It is hardly intrusive to see these plays as devices of psychological projection.

Of Barker's brief returns to the theatre, the chief one was the ten days he spent, at John Gielgud's invitation, attending rehearsals of the latter's *King Lear* production in 1940. Gielgud devotes a chapter to this experience in his autobiography *Stage Directions* and says: "[Barker] had only ten days to work with us on *King Lear*, but they are the fullest in experience that I have ever had in all my years on the stage." To read Barker's preface to *King Lear* is to read intellectual exegesis at its most practical, a theatre mind intent on exploring the text with performance as its imperative. To read the nine pages of notes that Gielgud made of Barker's specific suggestions for voice and movement—Gielgud gives them as an appendix—is to glimpse the theatrical gifts that underlay the essayist's gifts. To read both is to perceive the breadth of the man and the extent of the loss in his virtual retirement from a directing career at the age of thirty-eight.

In 1930, twelve years after their marriage, the Barkers moved to Paris. It was to be their place of residence, except for their exile during the Second World War, for the rest of their lives. Barker hyphenated his name to please his new wife, and they established themselves in a grand duplex apartment that had a staff of eleven. During the war they lived in New York, where Barker did some work for the British Information Service. He lectured at Yale, Harvard, and Princeton, and his book *The Use of the Drama* grew out of a series of lectures he gave at Princeton.

Before he came to America he had already become a legend, remote from almost all his former theatre associates, especially his former closest friends, the Shaws. In 1943 Shaw sent a postcard, one of his favorite literary forms, to Barker in New York: "Charlotte died last Sunday, the 12th September, at half-past two in the morning. She had not forgotten you. . . . You will not, I know, mind my writing this to you. She was 86. I am 87." Three years later Shaw wrote his obituary article about his former friend, twenty-one years younger.

Why did Barker leave? Why, before he had begun to reach the height of his one gift that can inarguably be called great, did he forsake the theatre? He sometimes answered that question. He wrote to Gielgud in 1937 that he had pinned his faith to the establishing of a permanent national theatre and "finding it . . . no go, I got out." He had said in 1915, rather wryly, "Since we cannot do away with the theatre, let us make it as good as we can." He had tried, in epoch-making fashion; but frustrated by the war and increasingly wearied by frustration, he finally allowed himself to be led away.

There are reasons beyond his theatre idealism, of course, that help explain his susceptibility to persuasion. "When Barker was young," says Purdom, "it was the thing to be a writer, while to be an actor was to belong to a despised profession. He never grew out of this

Experimenting with Shakespeare

I cannot regard every word that Shakespeare is supposed to have written as sacrosanct. He was not a perfect playwright; there can be no such thing. Moreover, he did not aim at perfection. . . . He aimed at vitality, and achieved it intensely. To vitality, then, in the interpretation of his work I would sacrifice preciseness. On the other hand, the plays have been so maltreated, both in text and construction, and we still remain so ignorant of their stagecraft, that our present task with them is, I think, to discover, even at the cost of some pedantry, what this stagecraft was. It may be that we can improve upon the original methods of their representation, but obviously we cannot until we know what these were. We must learn this, moreover, not in terms of archaeology, but by experimenting upon the living body of the play. For this purpose precise knowledge of the structure and usages of Shakespeare's own theatre will be as useful as a philosophic study of Hamlet's character may be inspiring. Neither, however, can tell us so much about the play as a play as its performance can.

—Harley Granville Barker, "The Player's Shakespeare," in *More Prefaces to Shakespeare*, Princeton, 1974.

Shaw was unhappy with Barker's 1913 production of Androcles and the Lion*: he thought the acting too restrained, and eventually turned the play into an extravaganza complete with gladiatorial duels. Above, the playwright brandishes a sword at Barker and Lillah during dress rehearsal.*

state of mind." He always preferred the company of other kinds of artists, of politicians and intellectuals, to that of people only in the theatre. There was certainly an appetite for misconstrued gentility in Barker that made him vulnerable to Helen's immense loathing of the workaday theatre. But fundamentally it was his inability to realize his visions that made him willing to give up.

In 1916 he even wrote a one-act play called *Farewell to the Theatre* about a famous actress who gives up her career because she cannot have it at the level she wants. That and his two subsequent full-length plays are his apologia in disguise. The history of the theatre contains other successful people who felt themselves cursed with theatrical talent, gifts they could exercise only in a place they disliked. William Charles Macready, the English actor, was an international star for three decades until he retired in 1851; the last two words of his voluminous diaries, after the entry noting his retirement, are "*Thank God!*" (Italics his.)

The tragedy of the English theatre was that it could not give the right home to an artist of Barker's vision. The tragedy of Barker is that he looked for the excuse to leave: that a residual Victorian ache for propriety aggravated his artistic frustration and sapped his will to fight further. And the tragedy is compounded because it is quite clear that in the library of his Paris apartment he was "directing" on paper, putting into his Shakespearean and other essays the force and wisdom that might have gone into the establishment of a history-making theatre.

The oddity is that he nevertheless did make history; that, despite his disproportioned career, he has had a huge influence, seen and unseen: on those who knew from whom they were learning and on those who learned from him whether they knew it or not. In 1967 the English critic Ivor Brown said, "Barker established the status and proved the value of the [director] in this country." In one way the statement is exaggerated; Barker was not the first. In another it is too modest; he also affected the United States—directly, by his productions and writings, but continuingly by the cultural osmosis that brings important artistic influences from England to America and vice versa. Whenever we see a director concerned with unity of concept, a company concerned with authenticity of style and the idea of a permanent ensemble, we can know that they are in some degree the progeny of Barker. Whenever we see a university supporting a professional theatre and professional training, we can know that the program is to some integral extent the result of Barker's *The Exemplary Theatre*. As for Shakespearean scholarship, few competent Shakespeareans would deny the vitality that Barker pumped into that body.

In his early play *Waste*, the young politician-hero, Trebell, objects to high-flown talk about the influence of God on man's search for knowledge and says that he wants to converse in prose. His opponent in discussion says, "What is the prose for God?" Trebell replies, "That's what we irreligious people are giving our lives to discover." The theatre proved too prosaic for Barker to discover his god in it, but before and after he left it, he did work that still helps those stubborn enough to hope.

Stanley Kauffmann contributes frequently to HORIZON. *A collection of his most recent essays,* Persons of the Drama: Theatre Criticism and Comment, *will soon be published by Harper & Row.*

THE CHINESE LANDSCAPE

Turning away from a bureaucratic, citified life,
the painters of the Sung dynasty created an unprecedented vision
of the natural world. For them, the mountain
was the message, and to understand the message is an art in itself

By EDMUND WHITE

THE METROPOLITAN MUSEUM OF ART; GIFT OF THE DILLON FUND, 1973

Landscape painting seems to us such an obvious and congenial genre that only with difficulty can we understand why it took so long to evolve. As Kenneth Clark has observed about the European tradition, "It is only in the seventeenth century that great artists take up landscape painting for its own sake. . . . Only in the nineteenth century does it become the dominant art, and create a new aesthetic of its own." It was the Chinese who first considered landscape as proper subject matter for painting, not as a backdrop or a setting for people but as a cosmos in itself—monumental, opened to infinite distances, untamed, dwarfing everything human.

Landscape became the "dominant art" during the Northern Sung dynasty (A.D. 960 to 1127), but it did so after more than a thousand years of the supremacy of portrait painting and historical and mythological scenes. In order for landscape to emerge as subject matter, the Chinese had to arrive at a highly refined attitude toward nature. That attitude was made up of equal parts of the urban dweller's yearning for rustic simplicity and the sophisticated philosopher's belief that virtue lies in attuning oneself to universal rhythms.

During the Northern Sung dynasty, many of the painters were members of the literati—that is, government civil servants who were also scholars. By tradition, there was no hereditary aris-

Summer Mountains, *a handscroll painted in the eleventh century, is a vast, richly detailed scene dominated by one huge mountain that towers in lordly splendor above lesser peaks. Apparent only on closer examination are minuscule huts at the water's edge, elegant pavilions tucked into hillsides, and antlike figures making their way along paths and over bridges. It is evening, and mist rises from the water as the fishermen at far right unload their boats. Probably a work of the artist Ch'u Ting,* Summer Mountains *is a rare example of the monumental landscape style that flourished during the Northern Sung dynasty.*

BOTH: PALACE MUSEUM, PEKING

Two of the owners of the handscroll on the preceding pages were the Sung dynasty emperor Hui-tsung, above left, sitting regally under a pine tree, and the eighteenth-century Ch'ing emperor Ch'ien-lung, who is examining works of art in his garden, above right. Collectors often wrote poetic appreciations on their paintings, and in 1748 Ch'ien-lung added such an inscription, in red ink, to the upper right corner of Summer Mountains.

tocracy to speak of; a man rose to eminence only by passing state examinations that tested his knowledge of the Confucian classics. Confucianism, with its emphasis on propriety and civic responsibility, made it perfectly suited to the stultifying world of officialdom. The Confucian classics had long been esteemed, of course, but it was only in the Sung dynasty that the civil administration was systematized along strict Confucian lines. Morality became synonymous with conformity to regulations that governed every aspect of life, from the clothes one wore to the manner of addressing the elder brother of one's father-in-law. Symptomatic of this static society is the fact that the favorite Confucian word, *li*, may be variously translated into English as "propriety," "good manners," "ethics," "politeness," "decorum," or even "worship," "respect," or "reverence." Certainly the ideal Confucian civil servant was nothing if not well-behaved—loyal to the emperor, faithful to the past, obedient to his superiors.

But China had another philosophical tradition every bit as ancient if not as orthodox as Confucianism, and that was Taoism. In Imperial China people were fond of saying a man was a Confucian in office and a Taoist out of office. Just as the worldly and status-conscious Romans were wooed by the spirituality and egalitarianism of primitive Christianity, so Confucian officials, numbed by the ceremoniousness of the state religion, sought refuge in the anarchic, anti-intellectual, eccentric, and highly individualistic tenets of Taoism. And it was Taoism that shaped the development of Sung landscape painting.

Lao-tzu—the supposed founder of Taoism and, according to legend, an older contemporary of Confucius—had despised civilization and idealized nature and its "way," the ineffable *tao*, the eternal spirit from which the universe sprang. Whereas a follower of Confucius would tend to be preoccupied with his scholarly work, a Taoist sage would keep to himself and do as little as possible. As the most important Taoist text, the *Tao Te Ching*, puts it:

In the pursuit of learning one knows more every day; in the pursuit of the way one does less every day. One does less and less until one does nothing at all, and when one does nothing at all nothing is undone.

So the Taoist sage—and later the Taoist-inspired painter—strove to do "nothing at all." By cultivating inaction, the painter believed he would come to serve as a simple conduit through which the vital force of nature could flow. It was characteristic for Taoists to say one should live according to *tzu-jan* (the spontaneous, the natural), not *ming-chiao* (the institutions and morals so favored by the Confucians).

Trapped in some provincial city or the imperial capital of K'ai-feng, a Sung government official would daydream about bamboo huts beside "mountains and water" (the words that in Chinese mean landscape). Whenever he was too weighed down by public and private responsibility, he could convince himself that at heart he was really a Taoist hermit, wandering through misty hills. And in his idle moments he would practice the three arts the Chinese of the Sung period regarded most highly, all closely connected with one another: calligraphy, poetry, and painting.

In an essay attributed to the tenth-century landscape painter Ching Hao, there is a dialogue between the young artist and an old Taoist sage. The sage asks, "Do you know the method of painting?" To which the artist replies curtly: "You seem to be an old, uncouth rustic; how could you know anything about brushwork?" The rustic, of course, knows a great deal, including the valuable distinction between painting a mere likeness and capturing the inner spirit of a tree or a rock: "Likeness can be obtained by shapes without spirit, but when truth is reached, both spirit and substance are fully expressed. He who tries to express spirit through ornamental beauty will make dead things." Again and again in the writings about art of the Sung, one finds passages that denounce the simple, mechanical copying of external appearances.

The covert target of such criticism may have been the Imperial Academy of Painting, which flourished under the emperor Hui-tsung (1082 to 1135). Hui-tsung, himself an accomplished artist, actively controlled the academy's production of realistic paintings of birds and flowers—to the neglect of pressing political problems. Though China was the wealthiest, most literate, most populous of nations, politically it was in danger. The empire was ringed by "barbarians." Particularly threatening were the aggressive nomads—the Khitan and Jurchen, the Tungus and Mongols in the north, the Mongols and Tangut in the northwest. But few of the emperors of the Northern Sung took much interest in military defense, preferring to devote their attention to the cultivation of the arts. When, in fact, the Jurchen finally conquered the capital, K'ai-feng, in 1126 and the court was driven south to found the Southern Sung, Hui-tsung could not take in the disaster and ended up a prisoner, presumably still fretting over minute aesthetic questions.

Impractical as the Northern Sung rulers may have been, their era must nevertheless rank as one of the high points in world culture. As the Sinologist Thomas Francis Carter put it:

The Sung Dynasty, shut out from the West by the steadily encroaching nomads, was a time of ripe maturity. Lyric poetry gave way to learned prose—great compendiums of history, works on natural science and political economy, of a character and quality such as neither China nor the West, except for a short period in Greece, had ever dreamed of. Religious faith gave way to philosophic speculation. . . . In art the lofty tradition of the earlier period was carried on and brought to fruition, so that the greatest and best Chinese paintings that are now extant come from the period of the Sungs.

The greatest paintings, however, the landscapes, did not always conform to the wishes of imperial patrons. Just as Americans today might accept grants from the National Foundation on the Arts and the Humanities but resist the strictures of official government taste, so Sung painters of integrity might enroll in the Imperial Academy, but clearly (if quietly) oppose its regulations. Less gifted academy members, decked out in purple robes with jade and gold insignia indicating rank, gathered in the imperial gardens and were examined by the monarch on their knack at rendering faithfully every feather of a pheasant or every petal of a flower. By contrast, in the best landscapes of the period there is a satisfying blend of natural observation and rebellious imagination.

That these two faculties, imagination and observation, were both respected by the Sung masters is clear in *The Great Message of Forests and Streams*, based on the sayings of the celebrated painter Kuo Hsi. He repeatedly emphasizes the need to probe the essence of a subject:

Whatever motif the painter represents . . . he should do it by concentrating on its essential nature. If something of the essential is lacking, the soul is not manifest.

But spiritual exploration of a subject should not take precedence over painstaking observation:

He who learns to paint bamboos places a stalk of bamboo in the clear moonlight so

"Mountains are immense things"

The thirteenth-century hermit dozing in his boat, above, is living a fantasy close to the heart of the Sung masters, who thought complete relaxation was the best preparation for painting. As the Sung dynasty painter Kuo Hsi put it, "He who devotes himself to the study of painting must above all empty his mind." Kuo Hsi, whose advice was later collected in *The Great Message of Forests and Streams*, had much to say about how painters should work and about landscape painting. Some excerpts:

- Men of the world think that pictures are made simply by moving the brush; they do not understand that painting is no easy matter. . . . The artist must nourish in his heart gentleness and cheerfulness; his ideas must be quiet and harmonious.
- Mountains are immense things. They rise and drop, open up and are seated; they should be expansive and massive, majestic and spirited and austere; they should look one way, should seem to raise their heads and to make a bow; . . . they should look up and look down over the valley, they should seem to come down and command those below.
- Streams are the blood veins of a mountain, the vegetation its hair, the clouds and mists its expression. Therefore, a mountain becomes alive with water, luxuriant with bushes and trees, and graceful with clouds.
- Wonderfully lofty and divinely beautiful are these mountains. In order to exhaust their marvels and grasp the work of the Creator, one must love their spirit, study their essential features, wander about them widely, satiate the eyes and store up the impressions in the heart.

OVERLEAF: *Once the inspiration of painters, these peaks "rise and drop, open up and are seated" above the Li River in south China.*

The airy pagoda in Buddhist Temple Amid Clearing Mountain Peaks, *attributed to the tenth-century artist Li Ch'eng, may have been a retreat for nature-starved city dwellers.*

that its shadow falls on a white wall; in this way the real shape of the bamboo comes out. He who learns to paint landscapes should not do it differently. He should go himself to the mountains and streams and contemplate them in order to grasp their aspects and meaning.

For Sung artists, painting was almost synonymous with religious meditation. In describing his father at work, Kuo Hsi's son wrote:

On the days when he was going to paint, he would place himself at a bright window before a clean table and burned incense right and left. He took a fine brush and the most excellent ink, washed his hands and cleaned the ink stone as if to receive an important guest. He let the thoughts settle in his soul, and then he worked.

Like all Sung painters, Kuo Hsi intended to transport the viewer into nature, but the scene was always a land of the imagination. Sung landscapes are never portraits of actual locales. Granted, a glance at a photograph will reveal a surprisingly close resemblance between parts of the Chinese terrain and certain landscape paintings; artists did not fantasize the odd, twisted shapes of weather-beaten pines or rain-eroded mountains that soar abruptly out of a flat plateau or lake. Indeed, painters were encouraged to sketch directly from nature. As Huang Kung-wang, a painter of the later Yuan dynasty, was to say, "The painter should always carry with him some brushes in a bag, then when he comes across startling trees in a beautiful landscape, he should at once make drawings of them so as to preserve their characteristics." But when the final painting was executed, the artist worked in his study, far from the scenes that had stocked his imagination. And what he painted was no identifiable monastery or waterfall or range of mountains, but a generalized, idealized composite of impressions he had gathered during his travels.

Perhaps because the visual impressions were recollected in tranquillity, there is not a single, consistent vantage point. Instead, the focal point moves with the moving eye of the viewer. This idealizing mental eye is also at work within each section, presenting each object, whether it be in the foreground, the middle ground, or background, as though it were seen from its "best," most recognizable angle. Even without realistic perspective, landscape painters succeeded in conveying a sense of great depth by overlapping surfaces and by resorting to atmospheric perspective—based on the principle that distant objects, dimmed by the atmosphere, are paler, cooler, grayer, and fuzzier. Indeed, each painting, despite its idealized locale, was specific about the season and the weather. As Kuo Hsi wrote, "Clouds and vapors of real landscapes are not the same at the four seasons. In spring they are light and diffused, in summer rich and dense, in autumn scattered and thin, in winter dark and solitary." This concern for atmosphere has worked its way into *Summer Mountains* (pages 86–87), recently attributed to Ch'u Ting, a painter of the Academy during the reign of Emperor Jen-tsung (1023 to 1056). According to a Sung critic, "In painting the changing aspects of landscapes in different seasons, and in his treatment of the melancholic and meandering mists and clouds and the movements of cascades and rocks, he showed considerable imagination and finesse."

The subtle effects achieved by the Sung painters are all the more remarkable because of the medium they worked in. Once ink is applied to absorbent silk or paper, it leaves an indelible mark. Mistakes cannot be corrected with a new coat as they can in oils. No second thoughts are permissible. In many ways, working with ink is like working with water colors, and in fact Chinese ink (or *mo*) was generally soot (pine soot was preferred) suspended in water and bound with liquid glue. The brushes, however, were more varied and pliable than any Western water colorist ever used. Rabbit hair was a favorite fiber, though the Sung painters Su Shih and Huang T'ing-chien were said to have favored wool and mouse whiskers.

The ink and brushes were exactly the same as those used by calligra-

NATIONAL PALACE MUSEUM, TAIPEI, TAIWAN, REPUBLIC OF CHINA — WANGO WENG

In Fan K'uan's eleventh-century scroll Traveling Among Mountains and Streams, *there are two small figures driving donkeys, and, in the hills above them, a half-hidden temple.*

Unrolling this handscroll. A Clear Day in the Valley, *in proper fashion, from right to left, a Chinese connoisseur could picture himself walking through the shady grove at right and perhaps entering the shelter in the clearing. There, in his imagination, he could sit for a while and contemplate the mountains. Continuing his journey, he might follow the shoreline to the spit of land at left center and, like the figures stopping there, look for miles, first one way and then another, at the wide expanse of river disappearing in the mist. Such vistas and delicate atmospheric effects were characteristic of the paintings of the late Southern Sung dynasty; this scroll, once attributed to the tenth-century artist Tung Yuan, is now recognized as a work of the thirteenth century.*

phers. In fact, similarities between calligraphy and painting abound. The *chung feng* brushstroke, for example, a common feature of calligraphy, is used to depict bamboo leaves. The point of the brush is held perpendicular to the paper. Gradual pressure is applied and released. The result is a beautifully shaped pointed stroke—or a leaf. Generally a poem in the upper right-hand corner of the painting is an integral part of the composition, as well as a comment on its subject. Painted or written scrolls were rolled and carried about in exactly the same way, and an admirable bit of calligraphy was displayed and studied with the same attention devoted to a landscape. Most important, a knowledge of calligraphy preceded the mastery of pictorial brushwork, and both writing and painting were judged as expressions of a man's cultivation and moral character. As one Sung landscape painter, known as "the Hermit of the West Lake," said: "I write in order to express my heart, I paint in order to satisfy my mind."

The image the Sung landscape painter transferred to paper or silk expressed perfectly his Taoist-inspired philosophy of nature. In the paintings, as in the philosophy, man fits easily into the environment, though only as a small instance of the universal energy that manifests itself more conspicuously in mountains and breathtaking gorges. The underlying unity the Taoist saw in nature is echoed several ways. First, there is the single color of ink. Whereas landscapes of earlier periods were rendered in bright colors, the effect of which was to isolate each object from every other, Sung landscapes are unified—both technically and spiritually—because they are virtually monochromatic. A gentle, overall illumination that indicates no single source of light is another unifying device, and so is the undulating rhythm of mountain peaks, culminating in one giant mountain.

That giant mountain is crucial. A close examination of Northern Sung landscapes, conducted by Sherman E. Lee and Wen Fong, has revealed that the order of construction followed by Sung artists consisted of "laying down first the skeleton of the 'host' mountain, then dressing the mountains with trees, horses, human figures and other details." This method to a large extent accounts for the massive, submerged strength and rational clarity we sense in the paintings of this period. In later

MUSEUM OF FINE ARTS, BOSTON

dynasties the order of composition was reversed. The difference was cited by a seventeenth-century critic: "Modern painters pile up small bits to make a big mountain, which is a great mistake. When the old masters composed large pictures, they made only three or four sweeping divisions and accomplished thus the whole composition."

The reputations of Northern Sung "old masters" are obscured by legend, and their works have been scattered, lost, copied, and recopied so many times that all attributions are questionable. Nevertheless, we can piece together some sort of rough history of the development of the landscape movement and its schools. The earliest painters were Kuan T'ung and Ching Hao, the very same youth who learned the *tao* of painting from the uncouth old rustic. The next generation was dominated by Li Ch'eng, perhaps the greatest of all Chinese landscapists, and he was followed by the early eleventh-century master Fan K'uan. (His one extant work, *Traveling among Streams and Mountains*, appears on page 93.) Both Li Ch'eng and Fan K'uan were regarded as superhuman creators, "in talent so exalted as to be beyond classification. . . ."

Li Ch'eng's *Buddhist Temple amid Clearing Mountain Peaks* (page 92) uses many of the devices characteristic of the Northern Sung landscape. The mist behind the temple and the larger mountain silhouette their details by lightening the backdrop, and mist girdling the base of a mountain obscures cluttering rocks and ravines, isolating the mountain as a separate entity. The rocks in the foreground are given character through careful texturing; the trees are spiky with "crab-claw" branches, an earmark of the artist's style.

Li Ch'eng's life was as inspiring to later painters as his landscapes, since he was the epitome of the withdrawn, scholarly artist who shunned public life. As his biographer wrote:

His grandfather and his father were both celebrated in their generation for their classical scholarship and their conduct of affairs. Ch'eng, however, had no other ambition than to lead a quiet life, and loftily declined all honors and advancements. In addition to being well versed in the canonical books and histories, he was a most excellent painter of landscapes. . . . His inspired versatility was the quintessence of the spiritual, very far beyond normal human capacities.

Li Ch'eng was from the north of China. Later generations viewed him and Kuo Hsi as the founders of a northern school, and the stark terrain rendered in the work attributed to them is characteristic of the Yellow River valley. By contrast, the landscapes of the tenth-century painter Tung Yuan and his pupil Chu-jan, who were both from the Yangtze valley in the south, are much looser, much more impressionistic. In the paintings of the later Southern Sung, such as *A Clear Day in the Valley* (above), the distant hills are lost in a sea of mist, and soft forms are built up in a profusion of dots. Conceptually, the technique represents a move toward greater abstraction and a more sophisticated perception of landscape as something mysterious and organic.

If nature was approached with reverence, so, too, were the paintings themselves. Even *looking* at paintings, Kuo Hsi averred, had to be done in the proper spirit: "If one looks at them with a heart of the woods and the streams, their value becomes great, but if one looks at them with proud and haughty eyes, their value becomes quite low." Connoisseurship had become so refined during the Sung that exhibiting a prize painting to a visitor was an elaborate ritual. Mi Fei, an eleventh-century collector and painter, described the extraordi-

nary precautions he took with a guest:

When Chancellor T'ang Chih-tung wanted to see my collection, I told him of my conditions. He agreed. I had two tables placed side by side and spread on them white paper and silk. I washed my hands and took out the scrolls myself from their respective cases and unrolled them for the visitor to see. He sat in front of the table with folded arms examining the scrolls with ease and care; when he said, "Open," I opened the scroll, and when he said, "Roll," I rolled. He sat there looking grand and dignified, while I ran about like a servant; and this I was willing to do in order to save my scrolls from being touched by his fingers and sleeves.

Above, a scholar whiles away the afternoon, lost in contemplation of a cloudy sky and haze-covered mountains much like those opposite. With only a few brushstrokes, Ma Lin, the thirteenth-century painter of this album leaf, has suggested an entire landscape.

The long, horizontal hand-scroll was an innovation of the Northern Sung, devised during the very period when landscape painting came into its own. Unlike the vertical hanging scroll, the hand-scroll tells a story of sorts, the narrative unfolding as the painted silk passes slowly before the viewer's eyes. *Summer Mountains* is only about three feet long and perhaps it was unfurled all at once, but *A Clear Day in the Valley*, a more typical scroll, is five feet long and a connoisseur would have looked at it in installments, working from right to left. Like film running from one spool to another, the painting would have been unrolled in segments, each about a foot and a half long. The "continuity" was provided by the interlocking mountain range in the distance, and the central climax was generally indicated by a huge, imposing mountain soaring to the very top of the painting. Often the end of the scroll was signaled by the strong vertical plunge of a waterfall or the soft dying away of hills.

Ideally, the viewer identified with one of the gnat-sized figures, the traveler on his donkey, for example, crossing a bridge in the right third of *Summer Mountains*. He is followed by his servant and appears to be making his way (the trip might take a day) to the elegant pavilions nestled higher up in the foothills in the left third of the composition. There he will join the microscopic gentlemen sitting before open windows and contemplating the awesome scenery; they may be laymen on a retreat at a monastery. Or, if the traveler is a mere merchant, he may take a turn to his left, traverse yet another bridge, and seek shelter in the rude huts depicted in the lower left-hand corner. As one Sung commentator said of the effect of such landscapes on the city-bound connoisseur: "You who but a moment ago were a common courtier or grubber in the dusty markets of the world are suddenly transformed." And Kuo Hsi wrote:

Contemplation of such pictures evokes in men corresponding ideas; it is as if one were among the mountains, and the scenery existed outside the imagination. When one sees the quiet streams and the setting sun, one feels like stopping in contemplation; when one sees the lonely men living in the mountains, one feels like staying there; when one sees the cliffs, the streams and the stones, one feels like rambling among them.

Not until the nineteenth century did Europeans approach nature with such reverence and affection. During the Middle Ages, forests and rivers, mountains and deserts—all were regarded as sinister and frightening. As late as the eighteenth century Casanova, while traveling through the Alps, drew the blinds of his coach so that he would be spared the sight of those vile excrescences of nature, the "deformed" mountains. From the charmed gardens of medieval tapestries to the formal gardens of Versailles, Westerners were determined to tame nature rather than worship it. Perhaps Christianity provided no means for comprehending and assimilating, much less appreciating, the unruly forces of the wild.

As Kenneth Clark remarked, only in the materialistic and scientific nineteenth century, as traditional religion was losing its hold over the Western imagination, did a new religion of nature provide painters with an aesthetic for landscape art. Believing that God was immanent in nature, they felt that landscape, in the hands of the truly visionary artist, could express His spirit. Once armed with this novel set of attitudes, they could finally turn to nature with the same passionate scrutiny that had so long before characterized the vision of the Sung masters.

Edmund White, author of Forgetting Elena, *often writes about the arts.*

ountains near Kweilin on the Li River

THE INVENTION OF POLITICS

The event occurred in ancient Athens when—much to the horror of the ruling elite—democracy first reared its head

By LIONEL CASSON

Democracy, "rule by the people," was created by the ancient Greeks, above all the Athenians. We like to think of those gifted people as governing themselves with the calmness of Socrates, the sober judgment of Plato. Not so. In its very infancy democracy developed the uncherubic features so familiar today—the machinations of pressure groups and manipulation of voters, the stuffing of ballot boxes, the excesses of soapbox oratory. Indeed, that is what Greek writers harp on: coming chiefly from the ranks of the well-born or well-heeled, they took a dim view of a political system that put them on a par with every Athenian Tom, Dick, and Harry.

For the Athenian style of democracy was democratic in the extreme. Imagine Rhode Island ruled not by a governor and state legislature but by a mass meeting of all male residents. Imagine its offices and commissions staffed not by elected or appointed officials but by citizens chosen by lot, and its courts presided over not by judges with the occasional help of twelve-man juries but by huge panels of Rhode Islanders picked haphazardly, at least several hundred strong and often several thousand. This was how the Athenians, who in fact inhabited an area about the size of Rhode Island, ran not only themselves but, eventually, an empire that stretched from Greece to Turkey.

Like all Greek states, Athens in its early days was under the sway of its aristocracy. As will happen, the poor grew steadily more unhappy with their lot, and by the sixth century B.C. tempers were near flash point. At the critical moment the celebrated Solon earned his immortal reputation for wisdom by coming up with a compromise that still left practically all political power in the hands of men of family and property, but opened the door a crack to democracy. Then, toward the end of the century, the door was thrown wide open: Cleisthenes, an ambitious Athenian with eminently proper aristocratic credentials, found he was getting nowhere with his own class, so he switched his efforts to the rank and file. They backed him with such enthusiasm that in 508 B.C. he ended up giving the city a liberalized constitution. Cleisthenes, then, was the founding father of Athenian democracy—but, like our founding fathers, he had not the faintest notion that the democratic seed he was planting would produce the luxuriant blossoms that flowered half a century later.

Most democratic governments today have three branches, executive, legislative, and judicial, each staffed by presumably qualified people. Athens had only one, the Assembly, and it was a strictly amateur operation, consisting of the citizens who managed to get there when a session was in progress. In the city's heyday, roughly the second half of the fifth century B.C., the population was about 300,000, but only some 50,000 adult males of Athenian parentage on both sides were voting citizens. (Women and children had no vote, and the rest—foreign residents, transients, slaves—no citizenship at all.) Each of the 50,000 was entitled to take a seat in the Assembly, listen to bills being read, add his voice to the debate, and shout or raise his hand when a vote was called. Actually only a fraction had the time or inclination to show up, perhaps some two to ten thousand depending on the agenda. Only the Assembly could make decisions, so it took up every conceivable kind of business, from declaring war to determining how large a salary a priestess of Athena should get.

The nearest thing Athens had to an executive branch was the Council, an arm of the Assembly that consisted of five hundred citizens over thirty who were chosen by lot. The Council met frequently, often every day. Its members prepared the Assembly's agenda, drafted bills, called meetings, saw to it that all decisions were carried out, and supervised whatever boards and commissions had been set up. A body of five hundred, to be sure, was handier than the Assembly with its thousands, but it was still a lot of people to get together. So, to provide a standing executive committee, the Athenians broke the five hundred down into ten groups of fifty, each serving for a tenth of the year, during which time they had to be on hand constantly. They had a special building in the agora, where they whiled away their spare hours, eating and drinking at state expense. Every day they elected one of their number chairman, and he spent the night as well as the day in the building. In effect, he represented the government during those twenty-four hours: he received dispatches, welcomed foreign envoys, alerted the Council in case of emergency, and, if the Council or Assembly met, he took the chair.

Like the Council members, nearly all officials were chosen by lot. Most served for only a year, and, since re-election was rarely permitted, the ambitious were prevented from getting a handhold on

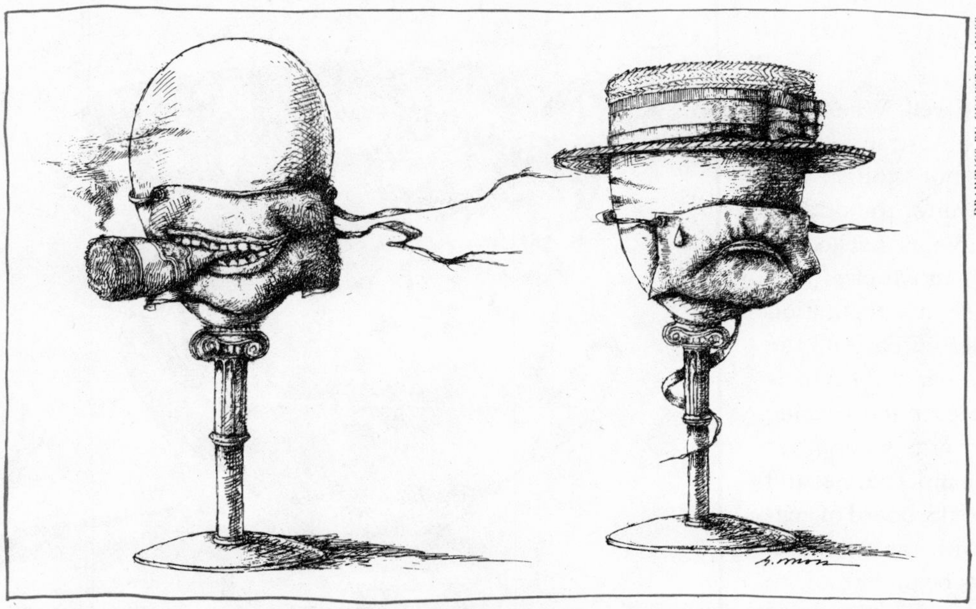

DRAWINGS BY GEOFFREY MOSS

Politicians in the classical mold: "The Athenian style of democracy was democratic in the extreme"

power. No matter that the routine of government was carried on by amateurs who were turned out of their jobs as soon as they started to get the hang of it all: the Athenians much preferred inefficiency to bureaucracy. There were few exceptions to this rule. The board of generals was one, or generals-admirals as we would call them, for they commanded on sea as well as land. War was too serious a business to be left to the lot, and generals were not only elected but eligible for unlimited re-election.

When Cleisthenes wrote his new constitution, he almost certainly supposed that the political leaders would be the same sort of men who had always led the state, men like himself, of pedigree and property. For the first twenty years or so he was right: the ones who ran Athens remained solidly aristocratic, and they were backed by their fellow aristocrats and prosperous farmers—the "useful people,"as Greek writers liked to call them. Then, in 490 B.C., and again in 480, Athens led the rest of Greece in the heroic resistance to Persia's attempts to invade the peninsula, and war, as it will, brought changes. Themistocles, a man of vision and canny political sense, came to the fore, and he hammered home the message that only a big navy could meet the Persian menace.

In Greece armies were cheap: soldiers were citizens who could afford suits of armor, and, when they marched forth into battle, each man packed along enough food of his own to last him a couple of days, by which time he was either a victor, a prisoner, or dead. Navies, on the other hand, cost money. First of all, there was the timber to import (Greeks were no ecologists and had so ruthlessly plundered their forests that by this time hardly any were left). Then there were the shipwrights to pay, and the fleet to maintain. Themistocles' social equals, army men all, were not interested in talk of a navy and so, like Cleisthenes, Themistocles turned to the rank and file, the tradesmen and artisans, fishermen and marginal farmers—the "useless people," as Greek writers liked to call them. He had so magic a way with them that, when a rich new vein of silver was discovered in the state-owned mines, he talked them out of dividing it among the citizens and instead into putting it toward the building of two hundred war galleys. His success set the aristocratic Establishment's teeth on edge, and a new political weapon emerged from the fray—ostracism.

Perhaps Cleisthenes included the procedure for ostracism in his original constitution; perhaps those who followed him added it as an amendment. We are not sure. At any rate, it took account of the possibility that the state would be better off if certain men could be quickly and easily gotten out of the way. (Having lived through the drawn-out drama of Watergate, we can appreciate that.) The procedure was as follows. At a meeting of the Assembly, a motion was put as to whether an ostracism should take place. If it passed, an Ostracism Assembly was called in the agora, and all who attended were issued an *ostracon*, a chunk of broken pot. (In an age that knew only expensive writing materials, potsherds were a standard form of scratch paper.) On his potsherd each voter inscribed the name of the man he most wanted to get rid of. Tally clerks counted all that were turned in to see if there were at least 6,000, the quorum required for an ostracism, and then went through them again to count names. The winner of this unpopularity contest had to leave the city forthwith and go into exile for ten years—without however, losing his property or civil status.

Whatever ostracism's original purpose was, politicians found it a useful way of disposing of rivals. Themistocles himself got his bitter enemy, the incorruptible Aristides the Just, ostracized. Ten years later, it was his turn. Not long ago archaeologists excavating a well on a slope of the Acropolis came upon almost two hundred *ostraca* inscribed "Themistocles," each written in the same handwriting. Obviously his opponents had prepared them for distribution, like the canned telegrams and letters we are handed today to send to our congressmen. Apparently they were not completely successful, and, to get rid of the *ostraca* that were left, they dumped them into the well. When they finally did manage to ostracize him, mere banishment was not enough: they condemned him as a traitor to boot.

The man the aristocrats backed to take over from Themistocles was Cimon. He had made his reputation through Themistocles' creation, the navy, which, shortly after the Persians were thrust out of Greece in 480, became Athens' major military arm. Cimon was a gifted naval commander; time and again he was elected to the board of generals and entrusted with the fleet, and whatever engagements he undertook he won. On top of being a glamorous war hero, he was gregarious, charming, and a born politician. As Plutarch relates:

"Themistocles set the aristocratic Establishment's teeth on edge, and a new political weapon emerged from the fray—ostracism"

> He took down the fences around his farm properties so that strangers and any needy citizen could go right in and pick the fruit. Every day he served a meal at his house, simple but plenty for a big crowd, to which any poor man who wanted could come. . . . A group of well-dressed young friends used to follow him around, and if he came across any citizen dressed poorly, one of these would change clothes with the fellow. . . .

But even Cimon's battle laurels and Tammany Hall techniques were unable to save him from the inevitable ostracism, though it took the greatest politician of them all to bring it off—Pericles.

The very opposite of the affable, hard-drinking Cimon, Pericles had the personality of a Charles de Gaulle and the political outlook of a Franklin D. Roosevelt. A scion of Athens' first family, he was so haughty and aloof that the Athenian wits dubbed him "Mr. Olympian." The reports are that he never laughed. He was a master orator, and in ancient Athens that was a key to political success. When he started in politics, Cimon was firmly entrenched as leader of the "useful people," and so Pericles, stiffnecked blueblood though he was, had to make his base the rank and file. It was to have revolutionary effects.

Once ostracism had gotten Cimon out of the way, Pericles, joining with another left-wing politician, Ephialtes, put through a series of reforms that set the city squarely on the road to full-fledged democracy. In theory the government was open to all citizens. In practice it was still in the hands of wealthy men, for governing Athens, like fighting in her defense, was something you owed her, not something for which you got paid, and the poor simply could not afford the time. Pericles and his followers pushed through a series of bills to provide pay for serving as magistrate or Councilman, for sitting on juries, for serving in the army or navy—not generous, but adequate. It was a giant stride to the left, and then they took another that raised even more aristocratic hackles: they stripped of its powers the one nondemocratic organ that Cleisthenes had allowed to linger on, the Areopagus, a judicial body with lifetime tenure and open only to men of property. This drove the opposition into hitting below the belt: since they could get nowhere on the floor of the Assembly, in baffled rage they had Ephialtes assassinated. Pericles himself rode out the storm and emerged as Athens' ranking political leader, a position he held until his death thirty years later, in 429 B.C.

"So long as Pericles headed the state, he led it on a moderate course and thus ensured its safety. Under him it was at its greatest." So wrote Athens' historian Thucydides, who grew up in the golden age Pericles created. The city's wealth and strength came from her control of an empire; the cornerstone of Pericles' foreign policy was to maintain that empire, and the cornerstone of his domestic policy, to build up the means for maintaining it, the navy. Athens' subject states paid compulsory contributions for the navy's upkeep. The total collected turned out to be more than was needed, so Pericles got the Assembly to allocate the surplus to a building program that adorned the city with the Parthenon, the gateway to the Acropolis, the temple to Athena Nike, and other structures whose fame has drawn tourists from his day to ours. This kept an army of masons, carpenters, painters, sculptors, and teamsters at work, while down at the waterfront another army of shipwrights, sailmakers, riggers, and stevedores was just as busy. The city boomed.

How did he do it? Only the Assembly had the power to authorize any actions, and considering its nature, it seems a miracle that any business got done, much less the program of a Pericles. The Assembly met in regular session only forty times a year, four times in each thirty-six-day period; meetings were necessarily adjourned when night fell, so the business on the agenda had to be disposed of by then. Those who asked for the floor addressed themselves, not, like today's legislators, to a manageable body of several hundred people used to working together, but to a motley mass of two to ten thousand with numerous different faces each time, all of them competitive, argumentative, voluble, hotheaded. There was no cloture, no Robert's rules of order—indeed, at times, no order at all. Socrates reports that if someone took the floor, someone "whom they do not think an expert, even if he's very much the gentleman, rich and from one of our best families, they will have none of him but jeer and boo until, shouted down in his efforts to speak, he either quits of his own accord or the Executive Committee orders the ushers to drag him away. . . ."

Pericles could not change the course of the ship of state in the slightest without first convincing this wayward, unwieldy body. Moreover, organized political parties did not exist in ancient Athens; like Themistocles' and Cimon's before him, Pericles' backing came from whatever voters happened to share his views. But Pericles had introduced pay for government service, and his building program had brought lucrative work to Athens' trades. The net result was that many more "useless people" were able to attend Assembly meetings and cast their votes for his motions. Then there were the rowers in the fleet. Lacking the price of a suit of armor to serve in the army, poor people had long been shut out of contributing to the defense of their state. When Themistocles persuaded Athens to start a navy, they too found a place—on the benches of war galleys, where all that was required was muscle. In Pericles' day, with the fleet's strength up to three hundred ships, each propelled by a crew of one hundred and seventy rowers, every citizen able to handle an oar was needed. As time went on these citizens became aware of their importance: the army might put on a fine show with its shiny breastplates and plumed helmets, but it was the naked rowers sweating on the benches who were the real source of Athens' imperial strength. They became a solid voting block that stood foursquare behind Pericles: what was good for the navy was good for Athens, and Pericles was good for both.

It was not only in politics that Pericles played the Olympian. Putting himself above Athens' social conventions, he divorced his highborn wife and took up residence with a famous courtesan, Aspasia, even having a child by her. Political cartoonists lay far in the future, but Athens had the equivalent in the writers of Old Comedy, a slashing free-for-all form of political farce, and Pericles became their pet target. He had a curiously shaped pate (thus, says Plutarch, his statues always show him with a helmet on), so their favorite name for him was "onion-head." They talked about Aspasia as if she were a madam running a brothel, and gleefully passed on the gossip that the sculptor Pheidias acted as Pericles' procurer. The great man was above it all. Plutarch tells how once someone followed Pericles about all day, pouring abuse upon him in the middle of the agora itself and even tailing him home; he took not the slightest notice until the moment he reached his door where, since it was dark, he called a servant to take a torch and light the fellow back to his house.

But as Pericles led Athens to an ever more commanding position, her neighbors watched with increasing anxiety. In 431 B.C. the inevitable clash broke out, the Peloponnesian War that Thucydides made so famous, and Athens found herself pitted against a coalition of Greek states led by Sparta. The conflict was to last twenty-seven years, until, in 404, Athens finally went down to defeat. During the war, the city, under a new breed of politician, would move ever further to the left.

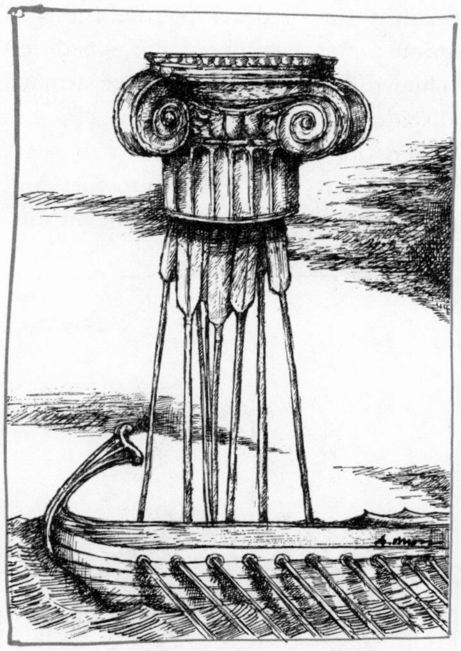

"The army might put on a fine show, but it was the naked rowers sweating on the benches who were the real source of Athens' imperial strength"

Pericles, in his statesmanlike way, had calculated the possibility of war and was ready for it. He had not, however, calculated the possibility of his own death. Two years after hostilities began, plague hit Athens and took the lives of thousands, including his own. In the midst of full-scale war, the political leadership, so long in Pericles' hands, was up for grabs.

For all their left-wing stance, Themistocles and Pericles had come from the traditional source of Athens' leaders, the aristocracy. The men who took over after Pericles' death were different. They were businessmen who had made enough money to enable them to go in for politics full-time. The first and best known, the bête noire of the "useful people," was Cleon, owner of a prosperous tannery; others were in lampmaking, cattle dealing, wickerware, flax. It was Cleon who first stepped into Pericles' shoes. Like his predecessor, he stood for maintaining the empire and the navy, but his technique was very different. "He was the first," Aristotle reports, "to yell when making a speech, to use abusive language, to tuck up his cloak when he addressed the people." Knowing he could not attract votes from aristocrats, he concentrated on the rank and file, introducing into Athenian politics the style of a Huey Long.

The upper crust of Athens had disliked Pericles, but the thought that the destiny of their city was now in the hands of a smelly tradesman—that was too much. Even the icily impartial Thucydides could not hide his distaste, and the writers of Old Comedy, who, like all ancient authors, were from the ranks of the "useful people," fairly foamed at the mouth. Aristophanes was exercised enough at one point to write a play, *The Knights*, given over entirely to reviling Cleon; in it he pits him against a salami peddler who outdoes him in yelling, lying, stealing, and fawning on the voters. The peddler boasts:

It was I who first went at that snaggle-tooth
monster,
though it meant my having to weather
a volley of threats in his barbarous Greek
and a sickening stink of leather.
He had eyes with the terrible flickering glare
of Athens' best known whore,
a cranium bristling with sycophants'
tongues,
a voice just like the roar
of a violent cascading stream that gives birth
to ruin wherever it falls,
the stink of a seal, the ass of a camel,
and the bogeyman's unwashed balls.

Most of the time the writers of Old Comedy used less vitriol and more wit. Here is Aristophanes' rival Eupolis:

Once upon a time
our generals used to be
the noble and the rich,
all men of pedigree.
We worshipped them. They were gods,
you see.
They had given us—security.

How different things are now!
When for a war we plan,
on leaders such as this
there seems to be a ban.
Instead we choose the kind of man
one finds in the city's garbage can.

Aristophanes and his fellow writers of Old Comedy portray Cleon, his political ally Hyperbolus, and their successors as vulgar and scheming upstarts, rascally nouveaux riches who bamboozle the common people. Thucydides thought it was the other way around, that Cleon and his like pandered for votes so vilely that they abdicated the role of leader and simply gave the mob what it clamored for: "The consequence," he wrote, "as one would expect in a great city ruling an empire, was a good many mistakes, including the expedition to Sicily." A few lines later, however, the historian remembers his judicious impartiality and sets about correcting the record:

Yet, even though they had lost the better part of the navy as well as other forces in Sicily, . . . nevertheless they held out for eight years against all the old enemies reinforced by new—by the Sicilians, by the majority of Athens' former subjects now in revolt from the empire, and ultimately by Cyrus, the Persian king's son, who furnished Sparta and her allies with the funds to build a navy.

Thucydides, however, does not mention the seventeen years preceding these eight, the seventeen years that followed Pericles' death in 429 B.C. When plague carried him off after nearly three decades at the helm, the ship of state did not suddenly begin to drift helplessly. The Assembly did not suddently act as if it had lost its wits, nor did the "useless people" badger their new leaders into drawing up laws to soak the rich. Quite the contrary: they co-operated with them to carry out Pericles' policies, and with no less success: the navy was kept up to the mark, the empire remained intact, contributions flowed in as before. What is more, Aristophanes hit his very peak, Sophocles and Euripides continued to write tragedies every bit as good as those composed when Pericles was alive, and no diminution of quality struck art, architecture, or sculpture.

In fact, Athens' first real setback came because it got so strong and wealthy that it developed delusions of grandeur and mounted the expedition Thucydides refers to, the huge armada dispatched against Sicily in 415 B.C. When that ended in defeat two years later, the city was still able to carry on. Cleophon, the foremost politician during the eight difficult years that followed, was another favored target of Old Comedy, but under his leadership Athens not only held out against the increasing odds that Thucydides describes, but even kept the building program going: the Erechtheum with the famous porch of the maidens was completed while a Spartan army camped not fifteen miles away.

"Pericles had a curiously shaped pate"—so the writers of Old Comedy quickly dubbed him "onion-head"

In recent years archaeology has turned up some new information about Cleon, Cleophon, Hyperbolus, and the others who got such a bad press. Cleon, for instance, though in the plebian business of tanning leather, was no nouveau riche; we know now that, thirty years before he made a mark in politics, his family was already in the charmed circle of Athenians wealthy enough to be regularly called upon for substantial contributions to the state. As for Cleophon, though he was in the equally plebeian business of manufacturing lyres, we know now that his father had been in politics before him and had actually been elected general. Hyperbolus was constantly jeered at for being not only a lamp manufacturer but an illegal immigrant, a dirty foreigner, and even, according to some, the son of a slave; we know now that his father was a perfectly legitimate citizen.

People often refer to the age of Pericles as an age of miracles. They have in mind Athens' superlative cultural accomplishments: it was the age when Aeschylus, Sophocles, and Euripides developed the art of tragedy, Aristophanes of comedy, Herodotus and Thucydides of history; the age when Ictinus designed that masterpiece of architecture, the Parthenon, and Pheidias decorated it with masterworks of sculpture. There is one more miracle of a different order to add to the list: it was the age when a miscellaneous mass of Athenians learned the discipline and responsibility required to run their state, history's first and last example of a body of citizens collectively and directly taking part in ruling not only themselves but a far-flung empire. And it was no flash in the pan, for it went on for a

"Aristophanes wrote a play given over entirely to reviling Cleon; in it he pits him against a salami peddler who outdoes him in yelling, lying, stealing, and fawning on the voters"

quarter of a century, until defeat in the the long-drawn-out duel with Sparta brought an oligarchical government to power and put an end to democracy.

The "useful people" of Athens, of course, did not see it that way at all. To them, the democracy they were observing in action was the ruin of their city. From our vantage point, however, we can see that, if there was a decline, it took Athens a good long while to hit bottom and that she enjoyed some splendid years before she did. And from our vantage point we can construct a totally different picture of what took place. After the plague killed off Pericles, the tradesmen and artisans and fishermen and dirt farmers who had made up his following were sufficiently disciplined to run their own show. They chose leaders whose backgrounds were like theirs, whose style was more suited to their tastes, who spoke their language. And they chose not ignorant and grasping upstarts but capable men from business families, men with the assurance and courage to address a public body that used crude and summary methods to show its displeasure. These men justified their choice by helping their following to carry on, through increasingly difficult times, the policies laid down by Pericles. Mistakes were made, but not as many nor as grave as their enemies claimed. The one that Thucydides singles out, the expedition against Sicily, cannot even be laid at their door. All classes voted enthusiastically for it, rich as well as poor, and the man most responsible for whipping up their enthusiasm was Alcibiades, a scion of Athens' very best family.

There is an anecdote told by Xenophon that is far more revealing than all of Aristophanes' badmouthing. Plato's brother Glaucon, when not yet twenty —which would place the incident in 408 or 407 B.C., the years of Cleophon's ascendancy—had visions of being a political leader. Each time he took the floor in the Assembly he would end up getting hauled off amid hoots and catcalls. His aristocratic friends and relatives were mortified, but no one was able to do anything about it until Socrates, meeting the young man on the street one day, slyly began to quiz him:

"Tell me now, what's the source of the state's revenues these days and how much do they amount to? Obviously you've looked into the matter. . . ."

"Lord, no! I haven't looked into *that*."

"Well, if you've overlooked that, you can at any rate give us the figure for the state's expenses. Obviously you have in mind to cut out nonessential expenses."

"Lord, no! I haven't given any time yet to that either. . . ."

"Then you can tell us the strength of our army and navy as well as of our enemies'."

"Lord, no! Not off the top of my head."

"Well, if you've got it written down, get it. I'll be glad to hear it."

"No. I don't have it written down either. . . ."

"Well now, I know you're concerned about national defense, and you know how many garrisons are strategically placed and how many are not, and how many troops make an adequate force and how many not, and you'll advise increasing the size of the strategic ones and eliminating the nonessential ones. . . ."

"Right! So far as I'm concerned, eliminate all of them. The way they do the guarding, the countryside gets robbed. . . ."

"How do you know they do a bad job of guarding? Did you go there yourself and investigate?"

"I'm guessing. . . ."

"But here's a point you of course haven't neglected but have looked into: how long the city can be fed on homegrown grain and what additional amounts are required annually. . . ."

At this point Glaucon could only sigh and observe, "It's an enormous job, if a man has to keep track of things like that."

Indeed it was an enormous job, but the citizens sitting in the Assembly needed such information to vote intelligently. Once upon a time aristocrats and prosperous yeomen had filled the benches and asked such questions; now it was the tradesmen, artisans, fishermen, poor farmers, rowers from the fleet. When a fancy-plumed, empty-headed whippersnapper had the effrontery to take the floor, they gave him short shrift and turned to someone like Cleophon because he knew the answers. This was democracy in the exact sense of the word, "government by the people," and it shares with Pericles the credit for Athens' finest hours.

Lionel Casson is professor of classics at New York University. His most recent HORIZON *article was "The Lure of the Vikings," in the Spring, 1975, issue.*

Queen Victoria and Her World

The political and social issues of our day have their roots in hers. She had opinions—*decided* opinions—about everything, from matchmaking to politics to the cosmos, some of them not so Victorian after all

DULWICH COLLEGE PICTURE GALLERY

Victoria first and last: above, in 1823, a princess of four; opposite, a queen-empress, seventy-eight, ready for her Diamond Jubilee.

Victoria Alexandrina first opened her round aquamarine eyes on May 24, 1819. Her earliest memory was of crawling on a yellow carpet in her mother's drawing room at Kensington Palace while over her reared the shadows of visiting bishops, grotesque in wigs and—horror of horrors—"*aprons*." Those large purple blots on a golden landscape might be taken for the whole fantastic chiaroscuro of her immense reign. It was long in time, longer still in change.

Her reign is, so far, the longest of any British monarch's: sixty-three years. She came to the throne at eighteen in 1837 and died in 1901 at eighty-one. Because of the country's energy and inventiveness, the scale of change matched the roll of time. The choice of examples is bewildering. Is it to be the advance in communications? Or the population explosion? The rise of the middle class? Or the growth of towns? Of slums? Why not begin with medicine?

The world of Victoria reached middle age, so to speak, with its archenemy still lurking unidentified, unknown. In the Oxford English Dictionary the earliest date given for the word "bacteriology" is 1884. When Victoria was young, fashionable doctors could think of no better panacea than bleeding, while the hopeful laity turned to magnetism and galvanism. Epidemics of cholera in the Tower of London were throught to be due to the sheer smell of its sewer moat. Similarly, when the prince consort died of typhoid in 1861, one theory was that the odor of soil turned over for the Great Exhibition buildings had killed him.

What a revolution by the end of Victoria's reign. London had been made "clean" despite itself by the public health reformer, Edwin Chadwick, and the queen, appropriately enough, made him a Knight of the Bath. Operations could be performed not only under anesthetics but also in antiseptic conditions. From both these discoveries the queen herself benefited. After the birth of her eighth child, in 1853, she paid lyrical tribute in her journal to the whiff of chloroform she had been given—only six years after it was first inhaled in Scotland. Dr. Snow, she wrote, "gave me that blessed Chloroform & the effect was soothing, quieting & delightful beyond measure." Her example advertised and sanctified its use, and later she met its pioneer, Dr. James Simpson, whose two assistants had passed out while making the first experiment. She also met Joseph Lister, the great surgeon who championed the use of antiseptics in 1865 and six years later lanced an abscess in the queen's arm. As she noted in her diary, Dr. Lister's "great invention" was "a carbolic spray to destroy all organic germs."

Or should the proud signal of change be penal reform? In 1820, the year after Victoria was born, condemned criminals were beheaded after being hanged; in 1902, the year after she died, Newgate Prison was torn down as being unworthy of its neighbor, St. Paul's. Meanwhile, the queen had admired Elizabeth

By ELIZABETH LONGFORD

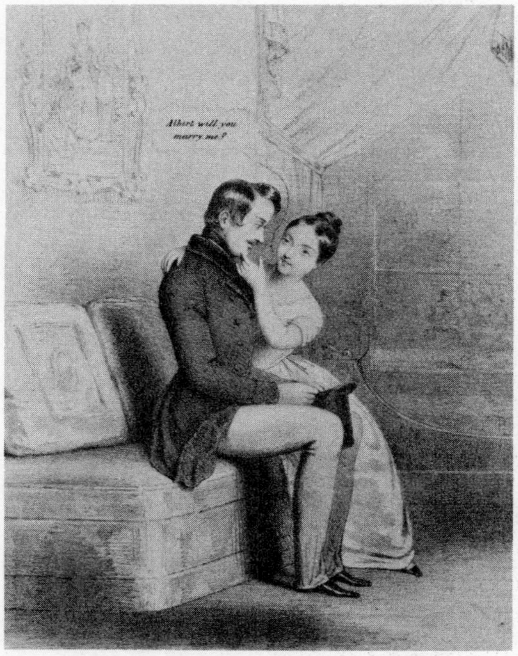

Lovers: the queen proposes to Albert

"Bertie," heir to the throne

Princess Beatrice in her cradle

Fry's prison reform work in the forties, the last convict hulk had sailed for the Antipodes in 1858, and the last debtors' prisons had been closed in the 1860's. Charles Dickens had helped bang the doors, remembering his own father imprisoned there, and re-creating him in Mr. Micawber. In 1870 the queen invited Dickens to the palace for a progress report:

> He is very agreeable with a pleasant voice and manner. He talked of his latest works, of America, the strangeness of the people there, of the division of classes in England, which he hoped would get better in time. He felt sure that it would come gradually. And I earnestly pray that it may.

Or must we go on twisting the extraordinary kaleidoscope of change until it comes up with the position and meaning of man himself in the universe? In 1853 Queen Victoria wondered in her journal why dinosaurs had become extinct. Six years later Charles Darwin gave the answer in his *Origin of Species*—giving rise to a new flood of questions far more poignant than the queen's casual query. "Survival of the fittest" was one thing, survival of the soul another. During the agonizing years following Albert's death, she found herself posing some of the key questions herself. "She asked me," wrote Randall Davidson, dean of Westminster, "if there ever came over me (as over her) waves or *flashes* of doubtfulness whether, after all, it might be all untrue"—"it" being the church's teaching on immortality.

The central decades of Victoria's world have sometimes been called the Railway Age. At the very moment the coaching system had reached perfection, it was ousted by steam trains. Those catching sight of an engine for the first time were inclined to see it as a kind of horse. Fanny Kemble wanted to pat Stephenson's "Rocket" like a pony, until the little beast ran over and killed the statesman William Huskisson. Princess Victoria saw her first train just four months before she came to the throne. The flying sparks she described could have come from its firebox or from hoofs:

> We went to see the Railroad near Hersham, & saw the steam carriage pass with surprising quickness, striking sparks as it flew along the railroad enveloped in clouds of smoke & making a loud noise. It is a curious thing indeed!

Victoria reflected the then common fear of travel by rail. "Not so fast next time, Mr. Conductor," said Albert after the royal couple's first train journey from Windsor to Paddington in 1842. The idea of corridor trains with "conveniences" dotted along their length did not occur to the early designers, and a public lion like the duke of Wellington complained bitterly about the crowds following him when he made a brief descent from his train at a station. Victoria, of course, did not suffer from this inconvenience, but even after corridor expresses were invented, she refused to use them, being allergic to speeds of more than fifty miles an hour.

Another advance in communications was the Penny Post, instituted in 1840 and unsung by the queen because her prime minister, Lord Melbourne, grumbled incessantly at its drain on the revenue. But the telegraph was an invention of which she made full use, especially in her battles with a later prime minister, Gladstone. Through telegrams she could communicate directly with her generals in the field, a right the cabinet disputed but the queen loudly claimed:

> The Queen always *has* telegraphed direct to her Generals, and *always will* do so, as they value *that* and *don't* care near so much for a mere official message. . . . The Queen *has* the *right* to telegraph congratulations and enquiries *to any* one, and won't stand dictation. She *won't* be a *machine*. . . .

Her wicked mastery of the telegram as a diplomatic weapon was further proved on the occasion of General Gordon's death at Khartoum. Gladstone's failure to rescue him was, Victoria felt, a crushing blow to the Empire's prestige, and she telegraphed him a rebuke *en clair* so that all the officials could read it.

Here was yet another vast change that occurred during the later years of her reign: the overwhelming growth of her imperium and imperial pride. Compare

"Believe me, children are a terrible anxiety"

When Queen Victoria and her cousin Albert fell in love in 1839, her superior status dictated that she, not he, should pop the question—as in the sentimental picture of the event opposite. Otherwise it was a conventional and happy match that produced a brood of nine, over whom the royal pair fussed and worried incessantly. They never managed to curb the mischievous tendencies of the Prince of Wales, who was to become Europe's favorite playboy. Nor did their plan for Beatrice work out: Victoria intended to keep her at home, but the princess found a husband anyway. Though the queen grumbled about what headaches children are, the royal family was very much united. They are, left to right, at Osborne House: Alfred, 13; Prince Albert; Helena, 11; Alice, 14; Arthur, 7; Victoria with baby Beatrice; Vicky, 17; Louise, 9; Leopold, 4; and the Prince of Wales, 16.

The royal family on the terrace at Osborne House, Isle of Wight, 1857

her sane and sober reaction to the horrific Indian Mutiny, which erupted in 1857 at the end of her first twenty years as queen, with her competitive frenzies of the eighties and nineties. Out in Cawnpore, young Captain Garnet Wolseley had reported that an "all-absorbing craving for ruthless vengeance" upon those Sepoys who had massacred English women and children "was deep in all hearts." All hearts? Certainly not Victoria's. Her instinct was that responsible people should try to forget the horrors and concentrate on winning Indian loyalty through humane government.

Believing that her Indian subjects were ill-treated, the queen at sixty-nine ostentatiously took a young Indian from Agra as an extra personal secretary, or "Munshi." Her court was scandalized. Equally scandalized was Her Majesty by their race prejudice:

> For them to make out that the poor good Munshi is so *low* is really *outrageous* & in a country like England quite out of place . . . She has known 2 Archbishops who were sons respectively of a Butcher & a Grocer . . . . The Queen is so sorry for the poor Munshi's sensitive feelings.

But if the queen opposed contemporary racism, jingoism was something she could share. Revenge against the Indian mutineers might seem to her un-Christian; revenge upon the Russian "barbarians" twenty years later filled her with the wildest excitement:

> I pitched into him [Lord Carnarvon, a minister urging moderation in the Russo-Turkish crisis] with a vehemence & indignation—who was at any rate inspired by the British Lion—& he remained shrinking but still craven hearted!—wishing to say to the world we cld not act!!! oh! that Englishmen were now what they were!! but we shall yet assert our rights . . . & "Britains never will be Slaves"—will yet be our Motto.

It was Disraeli who had fired the little volcano that many unwisely thought extinct. Deliberately laying on his flattery "with a trowel," he coaxed the mournful widow out of her seclusion at Windsor. To his credit, he had sold her the 1867 Reform Bill and then, more controversially, made her see herself as a queen-empress, dripping with Oriental gems and able at last to look the emperors of Russia, Prussia, and Austria in the face. As his "Faery Queen," she sent him gifts of spring flowers, ordering a wreath of primroses when he died, with the inscription "His Favourite Flower." Until the Victorian world disappeared, "Primrose Day" was celebrated every year by millions as a feast of Empire.

The queen's subjects were only too glad to enter into her imperial ardors. Both her Golden and Diamond jubilees were interwoven with imperial themes. Though the great-grandmother of Europe, who had supplied consorts for so many crowned heads out of her growing nursery, eccentrically insisted on wearing a bonnet for her Jubilee ride through London in 1887, to the cheering crowds her black bonnet was as imperial as any crown. And as for Britain's "position" in Europe, Victoria felt it had not moved, except, perhaps, upward, since Waterloo. When the Prussian government in 1857 requested that her eldest daughter, Vicky, the princess royal, travel to Berlin for her marriage to the Prussian crown prince, Victoria choked with patriotic rage:

> The assumption of its being *too much* for a Prince Royal of Prussia to *come* over to marry *the Princess Royal of Great Britain* IN England is too absurd, to say the least . . . Whatever may be the usual practice of Prussian Princes, it is not *every* day that one marries the eldest daughter of the Queen of England. The question therefore must be considered as settled and closed.

The marriage of Vicky at seventeen brought out all of Victoria's fears about sex. Like most girls in her day, the young queen had married with only the sketchiest idea of what to expect. So the queen inundated her daughter with her own phobias about marriage, man's sexual exploitation of woman, the trials of childbearing, and the disappointments of parenthood:

> Though I quite admit the comfort and blessing good and amiable children are—though they are also an awful plague and anxiety for which they show one so little gratitude very

GRANGER COLLECTION

"Invaluable" John Brown

"Faithful old servants"

On the subject of race and class, Victoria was virtually a radical. "That division of classes," she wrote, "is the one thing . . . most dangerous and reprehensible." With two of her servants—the bluff Highlander John Brown and her Moslem secretary, the "Munshi"—she practiced what she preached. After Albert's death, Victoria and Brown became boon companions, to the scandal of the court and nation, and she stoutly defended the Munshi against all kinds of slurs, racial and otherwise.

BY GRACIOUS PERMISSION OF HER MAJESTY QUEEN ELIZABETH II

Signing state papers about 1898; at left, the Munshi

often! What made me so miserable was—to have the two first years of my married life utterly spoilt by this occupation! I could enjoy nothing [nor] go about with dear Papa and if I had waited a year, as I hope you will, it would have been very different.

A few weeks later, the queen heard that Vicky was, in fact, pregnant:

What you say of the pride of giving life to an immortal soul is very fine, dear, but I own I cannot enter into that; I think much more of our being like a cow or a dog at such moments; when our poor nature becomes so very animal & unecstatic.

Curiously enough, eighteen years earlier, Queen Victoria had apparently shocked her *accoucheur*, Dr. Charles Locock, by the frank prenatal inquiries she made when Vicky was on the way. "Every Medical observation which she made," reported Locock to his friend Lady Mahon (who passed on the gossip until it eventually reached the duke of Wellington), "& which might perhaps bear two significations, was invariably considered by Her Majesty in the least delicate sense. She had not the slightest reserve & was always ready to express Herself, in respect to Her present situation, in the very plainest terms. . . . She goes without stays or anything that keeps Her shape within bounds. . . . She is more like a barrel than anything else."

Eighteen years later, this robust creature had vanished. The queen had taken to stays with a vengeance and was sending Vicky advice on how to use her gift of two pairs. Never lace them tight—but lace them—and change them for a larger pair every six weeks or two months, writing on the discarded pair the date. "It is of great use—hereafter."

Accused of indelicacy at twenty-one, the queen in her forties was in the grip of mid-Victorian prudery, as were her admirers. Beloved Albert had had a great success in cleaning up the court, and Lord Shaftesbury, a strict evangelical churchman and champion of progressive factory acts, told the queen her model family life was universally approved.

As for prudery, it seemed as acceptable to the middle classes as to the queen herself. When she was in her fifties, customs began to relax again among the upper classes, but the queen stuck resolutely to a prudish line:

The animal side of our nature is to me—too dreadful & now—one of the new fashions of our elegant society, is to go in perfectly light-coloured dresses—quite tight—without a particle of Shawl or Scarf (as I was always accustomed to wear & to see others wear,)—& to dance within a fortnight of the confinement even valsing at 7 months!!! Where is delicacy of feeling going to!

William Cobbett, the pre-Victorian radical writer, once said that he would not consider delicacy to have increased in England until the streets ceased to swarm with prostitutes and the mansions of the aristocracy with bastards. It was particularly the raging incidence of Victorian prostitution that convinced so many realists that the great age of middle-class morality was, in effect, a paradise for hypocrites.

Despite her adoration of Albert, the queen took the typical Victorian view that Man was basically a monster:

Yes, dearest [she wrote to Vicky in 1859], it is an awful moment to have given one's innocent child up to a man, be he ever so kind and good . . . it is like taking a poor lamb to be sacrificed . . . I know that God has willed it so and that these are the trials which we poor women must go through; no father, no man can ever feel this! Papa never would enter into it all!

After hearing from Vicky how badly Prince Frederick Charles of Prussia was treating his wife, the queen launched into a violent tirade:

That despising our poor degraded sex—(for what else is it as we poor creatures are born for man's pleasure and amusement . . .) is a little in all clever men's natures . . . dear Papa even is not quite exempt though he would not admit it—but he laughs and sneers constantly at many of them and at our unavoidable inconveniences, etc., though he hates the want of affection.

How far did the queen wallow in her sex's "degradation" rather than strive to

Viscount Melbourne

Viscount Palmerston

RADIO TIMES HULTON PICTURE LIBRARY

Benjamin Disraeli, democratic Tory

CAMERA PRESS

W. E. Gladstone, Liberal

"*How* proud I feel to be Queen of *such* a Nation"

So wrote the young sovereign in 1838. Though her political power was limited, she attentively rode herd on a long succession of prime ministers. They included Lord Melbourne (her kindly surrogate father), Palmerston (he inspired her now with horror at his womanizing, now with admiration for his grasp of European politics), Disraeli (he called her the "Faery Queen"), and Gladstone (she called him a humbug and heartily disliked him).

liberate it? There seems to have been a touch of masochism somewhere, for when women's rights movements developed, they were almost always met by a glare from the throne. True, she would also inveigh against marriage:

> I am equally shy of marriages & large families . . . better a 1000 times never marry, than marry for marrying's sake, wh I believe the gter number of people do.

But the idea of women entering the professions appalled her. Nursing was an exception. She honored Florence Nightingale deeply, describing her as gentle, ladylike, systematic, neither puffed up nor falsely humble. "I envy her being able to do so much good & look after the noble brave [Crimean] heroes whose behaviour is admirable." But she hotly opposed medical degrees for women:

> What an *awful* idea this is—of allowing *young girls* & young men to enter the dissecting room together. . . . This mad wicked folly of women's rights . . . is a subject which makes the Queen so furious that she can't contain herself.

As for Lady Amberly (Bertrand Russell's mother), who wanted to get women the vote, she needed a whipping.

The queen enjoyed her most delicious paroxysms of self-abasement after Albert's triumph in organizing the Great Exhibition of 1851. His Palace of Glass, dedicated to international trade and brotherhood, glittered like the Koh-i-Noor diamond in the forehead of Victorian England. "Albert's dearest name is immortalised with this *great* conception, *his* own," she rhapsodized. "We women are not *made* for governing—& if we are good women, we must *dislike* these masculine operations."

Nevertheless, if either of them governed, it was Victoria, not Albert. Or was the throne already a powerful symbol rather than an instrument of government? The poor queen worked herself up into many unnecessary tantrums over her failure to alter political trends. Her sphere was tacitly limited to the right, as Walter Bagehot defined it, "to be consulted, to encourage and to warn." Yet her duty as she saw it was to stem the tide of democracy:

> The Queen is as sincerely a liberal in her views for the improvement of her Empire as anyone can be, but . . . she *cannot* and will not be the Queen of a *democratic monarchy*; and those who have spoken and agitated . . . in a very radical sense must look for *another monarch*; and she doubts if they will find one.

In fact, there was not all that much democracy in Victorian England, and it was really the means to achieving it that inflamed her. She especially disliked Prime Minister Gladstone's "Royal Progresses," as she called his whistle-stop election tours of Scotland. "The Queen is *utterly* disgusted with his *stump* oratory—so unworthy of his position—almost under her very nose." In desperation she begged Lord Tennyson to expostulate with the Grand Old Man. "Can you not have some influence with Mr Gladstone in preventing him making another round of agitation in the autumn?" Deeply embarrassed, the poet approached the statesman—and got nowhere. "Mr Gladstone goes no further than to say he will not if he can help it." But he could not help it. Democracy was a more persuasive taskmistress than the old queen, and Gladstone, whom she now called "this half crazy & really in many ways ridiculous old man," duly carried out another successful wooing of the electorate. She never forgave him his nickname—"The People's William."

Like the majority of her subjects, the queen was essentially pragmatic in her approach to art. The story of her son Prince Arthur and the duke of Wellington's casket illustrates perfectly this Victorian attitude. On young Arthur's first birthday the duke presented his godson with a gold cup and a model of the throne. Albert decided to have this moving occasion painted by Winterhalter, but substituted a casket for the duke's actual presents. When Prince Arthur grew up, his friends badgered him to tell them what was in the mysterious casket. Surely something thrilling, to be opened when he was twenty-one? At last Arthur begged his mother to enlighten him—and received the following reply:

"Homage to Queen Victoria," Osborne House, 1888

"We women are not *made* for governing"

Though deeply conscious of the indignities visited on her sex by nature (e.g., childbirth) and male domination, Victoria was no feminist. She had her notions about proper feminine behavior and was not shy about enforcing them. In the tableau vivant *at left, a group of her ladies-in-waiting crowns a bust of the queen. One can be sure that they lived up to Her Majesty's standards: those who did not were harshly served. When Lady Flora Hastings, unmarried, was falsely accused of being pregnant, the queen shunned her mercilessly. (Lady Flora died soon after of a tumorous liver.) Mrs. Disraeli, whose morals were above reproach, failed nevertheless to impress Victoria ("*She *is very vulgar . . . in her way of speaking"). Yet of Florence Nightingale, Victoria could say: "I envy her being able to do so much good."*

Darling Arthur, I hasten to answer your letter recd this mg by a *most positive denial*, as to the casket. It is *utterly* without any foundation . . . & I cannot imagine *how* such a *story* cd be invented; except that perhaps as in the fine Picture . . . the Duke holds a box up to you—and people imagined it was a casket containing something.

The simple fact was that dear Papa wished the picture to represent "*an Event*," as Rubens and Veronese did in "*Periods of History*," and felt that something more picturesque than the duke's gifts should be put into his hand, which would equally well tell the story. So dear Papa substituted "a pretty box," which he had himself once given to Mama, for the duke's real gifts:

These are the facts. . . . I *wish* it had been otherwise. But it only shows how *wrong* in fact it is not to paint things as they really are.

"Things as they really are . . ." The queen could not abide the "greenery-yallery" aestheticism that W. S. Gilbert satirized in *Patience*. She would not be painted by G. F. Watts for fear of getting "green flesh and blue lips," nor by Sir John Millais after his behavior while painting Ruskin's wife Effie. She heard that Millais had seduced Mrs. Ruskin before marrying her himself—a risk that apparently alarmed the queen!

Apart from the problems that the queen and the stolid middle classes thus raised for the art world, how far did they face "things as they really are" in the world of people? Looking down from her golden throne, did Victoria notice that large tracts of Britain were as black as pitch? The horrors of industrial landscapes were by no means absent from her journals, as they were from those of most gentlewomen:

It is like another world. In the midst of so much wealth, there seems to be nothing but ruin. As far as the eye can reach, one sees nothing but chimneys, flaming furnaces, many deserted but not pulled down, with wretched cottages around them & heaps of the refuse & dross of the metal which has been worked. They have the effect of gigantic molehills. Add to this a thick & black atmosphere, & a few miserable trees, on which no leaves can live, & you have but a faint impression of the life, under these circumstances, which a 3rd of a million of my poor subjects are forced to lead. It makes me sad!

Victoria was right to speak of "another world," but she could not know that in the Black Country of 1852 she was observing only the tip of the iceberg, nor that beneath the surface bubbled a vast underworld of crime and vice. Here the "indelicacy" that she saw and deplored aboveground flourished as pornography, to be recorded by the anonymous Victorian diarist in the pages of *My Secret Life*. Nor could she suspect the strange way in which another of her subjects would break out from sexual taboos and the class-ridden Victorian cage. The diaries of Arthur J. Munby, published in 1972 as *Munby, Man of Two Worlds*, describe the astonishing fixation of an honorable and sensitive Victorian, a friend of Ruskin and Rossetti, upon toil-worn workingwomen, culminating in his marriage with Hannah, a housemaid.

The queen often criticized her class-ridden German relatives-by-marriage for not visiting the poor in their homes, as English ladies did. She herself believed in the personal touch. Continental social services, however, certainly did not lag behind British ones, and when Gustave Doré came to London and drew its portrait he was careful to show the dark as well as the light: the prison yard, the treadmill, Westminster as a backdrop to the city's worst square mile of squalor, and a glorious St. Paul's shining above a wilderness of chimneys.

The type of "poor" with whom the rich were most at home were, of course, domestic servants. According to the 1851 census, this was the second-largest group of workers in Britain, ranking only after farmers. Unfortunately, the queen's genuine concern for her own domestic staff probably did more to annoy her family than to set her foreign relations a good example. In 1868 she ordered Lord Charles Fitzroy, her Master of the Household, to drop a hint to her son-in-law about staying up late in the smoking room at Balmoral:

"Poor" Lady Flora Hastings

NATIONAL PORTRAIT GALLERY, LONDON

"Very vulgar" Mrs. Disraeli

"Noble" Florence Nightingale

LEFT AND RIGHT: GRANGER COLLECTION

Lord Charles would perhaps simply mention to Prince [Christian] *without* giving it as a *direct order* that the Queen felt it *necessary* for the sake of the *servants*, who were kept up so late and who had to be up so early in the morning, to direct that the smoking room should be closed and the lights put out by *12* o'clock—*not* later.

Everyone knew that this ukase was for the benefit of her personal servant, John Brown, that archetypal pampered domestic favorite found in so many great houses over the centuries. That Brown was something more to the queen might well seem indicated by the reminiscences she sent to his brother Hugh after faithful John's death:

Dear John said to me, "I wish to take care of my dear good mistress till I die. You'll never have an honester servant." I took and held his dear kind hand and said I hoped he might long be spared to comfort me.... Afterwards my beloved John would say: "You haven't a more devoted servant than Brown"—and oh! *how* I felt *that*! Afterwards so often I told him no one loved him more than I did or had a better friend than me: and he answered "Nor you—than me. No one loves you more."

Yet despite the scandal, it is highly improbable that she was John's "dear good mistress" in any but the most guileless sense—and she certainly was not "Mrs. Brown." It is perhaps not overfanciful to see a link, however tenuous, between Victoria's affection for her John and Munby's for his Hannah. A relationship with a rough, handsome servant may have been commoner than we imagine among Victorians who were lonely and understandably troubled about sex.

The death of Prince Albert strained the queen's spiritual resources to the breaking point. At a time when the "higher criticism" of the Bible was being given teeth by Darwin's theory of evolution, she found little consolation in the Anglican Church, preferring Presbyterianism: "I do not like bishops . . . I like the man but *not* the bishop." During her neurotic seclusion after Albert's death, she ran the risk of losing not only her people's affection but her own faith. Some people, however, reveled in her tear-stained constancy. A cook who worked near the Albert Memorial loved to see Her Majesty drive up daily and weep for a few minutes into a black-bordered handkerchief.

It was Tennyson more than anyone else who gave her faith the twist it needed. Mourning his lost friend, Arthur Hallam, he wrote *In Memoriam*, expressing his hard-won belief that the dead went through a kind of spiritual evolution. "*They* do not sleep," he said of the dead—which exactly suited the queen's hopes of an energetic afterlife. His line in the dedication to the *Idylls of the King* was responsible for her only known psychic experience: "Break not, O Woman's heart, but still endure." Once when feeling suicidal, she heard a mystic voice saying, "Still endure." Though she probably did not realize it, the voice was Tennyson's. From him she also learned to see death as a white not a black event, and she copied him in ordering for herself a "white funeral." Curiously enough, however, she sent an enormous wreath of jet-black laurel leaves for Tennyson's grave. The truth was that Victoria was too much a child of her time to escape "the Victorian way of death." But at least she made the effort.

Taking a wider view of her and her world, she was also typically Victorian in the contradictions that Freud has brought to light. Psychoanalysis finds that overweening self-confidence is usually a sign of hidden anxieties. Victoria undoubtedly concealed a palpitating heart beneath the formidable exterior. In this she surely represented her age. Compact of powerful, ponderous well-being, her world already felt in its bones the damp, raw air of change. At her passing, those fears rose to the surface and broke in huge waves of tribal grief.

Elizabeth, countess of Longford and queen mother of the Longford-Pakenham-Fraser family of authors, is the biographer of Victoria, the duke of Wellington, and, most recently, Churchill.

"Ever your devoted Grandmama, V.R.I."

BY GRACIOUS PERMISSION OF HER MAJESTY QUEEN ELIZABETH II

In Coburg to attend a wedding, Queen Victoria posed for this portrait with part of her family on April 18, 1894.

1 H.R.H. Beatrice of Saxe-Coburg**
2 H.R.H. Feodora of Saxe-Meiningen
3 Kaiser Wilhelm II**
4 Queen Victoria
5 Empress Victoria of Germany*
6 Prince Alfred of Saxe-Coburg**
7 Nicholas, the czarevitch
8 H.R.H. Alix of Hesse**
9 H.R.H. Victoria of Battenberg**
10 H.R.H. Irene of Prussia**
11 Grand Duchess Marie of Russia
12 Marie, duchess of Saxe-Coburg
13 Edward, Prince of Wales*
14 H.R.H. Beatrice of Battenberg*
15 H.R.H. Louise of Saxe-Coburg
16 H.R.H. Alexandra of Saxe-Coburg
17 H.R.H. Charlotte of Saxe-Meiningen**
18 Louise, duchess of Connaught
19 Prince Louis of Battenberg
20 Prince Henry of Battenberg
21 Grand Duke Sergius of Russia
22 Prince Ferdinand of Romania
23 Grand Duke Vladimir of Russia
24 Arthur, duke of Connaught*
25 Grand Duke Paul of Russia
26 Prince Philip of Saxe-Coburg
27 Count Mensdorff
28 H.R.H. Marie of Romania**
29 Grand Duchess Elizabeth of Russia**
30 Alfred, duke of Saxe-Coburg*

*First generation
**Second generation

They are all gone now, and all their crowns but one. Yet in 1894, when the aging queen sat for this portrait with some of her children and grandchildren, they seemed about to possess every throne of Europe. Victoria Regina et Imperatrix (4) looks glum: she had just learned that her granddaughter Alix (8) was engaged to Nicholas (7), the czarevitch. Russia, as Victoria wrote, was a nation "so rotten that at any moment something dreadful might happen." Alix's sister Elizabeth (29) had already wed (against Grandmama's wishes) a Russian grand duke—Sergius (21).

The "something dreadful" bided its time. Sergius was assassinated in 1905; in 1918 Nicholas and Alix—renamed Alexandra—and their children faced the firing squad at Ekaterinburg. Elizabeth died that same year, thrown down a mine shaft by Bolshevik partisans. Genetic tragedy also lurks behind the photograph; for Victoria carried the gene for hemophilia, as did her daughters Beatrice (14), Alice (not pictured), and Vicky (5), though Vicky's son Kaiser Wilhelm II (3) managed to escape the heritage. And, of course, Alix was also a carrier. The most famous victim was her son Alexis, the last czarevitch, whose affliction—some say—led to the downfall of the Romanov dynasty. But not all these royal children came to grief. We see a future king of Romania, Ferdinand (22), and his queen, Marie (28)—it was hardly a steady job but at least no firing squad arrived. Victoria of Battenberg (9) lived to see her own grandson married to the present queen of England, who is herself a great-great-grandchild of the grandmother of Europe.